T0316566

Cambridge Elements ⯠

Elements in the Archaeology of Europe
edited by
Manuel Fernández-Götz
University of Edinburgh
Bettina Arnold
University of Wisconsin–Milwaukee

ARCHAEOLOGY OF THE ROMAN CONQUEST

Tracing the Legions, Reclaiming the Conquered

Manuel Fernández-Götz
University of Edinburgh

Nico Roymans
Vrije Universiteit Amsterdam

European Association
of Archaeologists

CAMBRIDGE
UNIVERSITY PRESS

Shaftesbury Road, Cambridge CB2 8EA, United Kingdom

One Liberty Plaza, 20th Floor, New York, NY 10006, USA

477 Williamstown Road, Port Melbourne, VIC 3207, Australia

314–321, 3rd Floor, Plot 3, Splendor Forum, Jasola District Centre,
New Delhi – 110025, India

103 Penang Road, #05–06/07, Visioncrest Commercial, Singapore 238467

Cambridge University Press is part of Cambridge University Press & Assessment,
a department of the University of Cambridge.

We share the University's mission to contribute to society through the pursuit of
education, learning and research at the highest international levels of excellence.

www.cambridge.org
Information on this title: www.cambridge.org/9781009507295

DOI: 10.1017/9781009182003

First published 2024

A catalogue record for this publication is available from the British Library.

ISBN 978-1-009-50729-5 Hardback
ISBN 978-1-009-18199-0 Paperback
ISSN 2632-7058 (online)
ISSN 2632-704X (print)

Archaeology of the Roman Conquest

Tracing the Legions, Reclaiming the Conquered

Elements in the Archaeology of Europe

DOI: 10.1017/9781009182003
First published online: February 2024

Manuel Fernández-Götz
University of Edinburgh

Nico Roymans
Vrije Universiteit Amsterdam

Author for correspondence: Manuel Fernández-Götz,
M.Fernandez-Gotz@ed.ac.uk

Abstract: This Element volume provides an up-to-date synthesis of the archaeology of the Roman conquest, combining new theoretical and methodological approaches with the latest fieldwork results. Recent advances in conflict archaeology research are revolutionising our knowledge of Rome's military campaigns in Western and Central Europe, allowing scholars to reassess the impact of the conquest on the indigenous populations. The volume explores different types of material evidence for the Roman wars of conquest, including temporary camps, battlefields, coinage production, and regional settlement patterns. These and other topics are examined using four case studies: Caesar's Gallic Wars, the Cantabrian and Asturian Wars, the Germanic Wars of Augustus, and the Roman conquest of Britain. By focusing on the 'dark sides' of the Roman expansion and reclaiming the memory of the conquered, the Element aims to contribute to a more holistic understanding of the processes of incorporation and integration into the Roman Empire.

Keywords: Roman conquest, Gallic Wars, Cantabrian and Asturian Wars, Germanic Wars, Conquest of Britain.

ISBNs: 9781009507295 (HB), 9781009181990 (PB), 9781009182003 (OC)
ISSNs: 2632-7058 (online), 2632-704X (print)

Contents

1 Introduction

1.1 Scope and Aims

The Roman conquest, i.e. the annexation of new territories by the expanding Roman state, was one of the most important processes of the ancient world. Starting as a relatively small city-state in central Italy, over the course of several centuries Rome gradually expanded its dominion to the point that by the second century AD it extended from the Atlantic coast of Iberia to the Near East, and from northern Britain to the Sahara (Morley 2010; Woolf 2022) (Figure 1). A vast body of literature by both ancient historians and archaeologists documents the multiple military campaigns and strategies that were employed in order to incorporate new territories (e.g. Badian 1968; James 2011; Maschek 2021). The Roman military has been an attractive field of study since at least the nineteenth century, and it continues to captivate the interest of scholars and the public alike. This is reflected not only in academic publications, but also in popular books, museums, and re-enactment groups.

Why, then, do we need a new publication on this topic, and what makes this volume different? While we do not claim to present data that are completely novel, our aim has been to produce an up-to-date overview of Rome's military conquest campaigns in the West, summarising a large amount of information in combination with a theoretically informed approach and some original interpretations. This is a timely moment for this task. The last few decades have witnessed an enormous increase in the quantity and quality of archaeological evidence related to various Roman wars of conquest (e.g. Fitzpatrick and Haselgrove 2019; Roymans and Fernández-Götz 2019). More widely, the rapid development of conflict archaeology as a field of study that increasingly engages with the prehistoric and early historic periods (Dolfini et al. 2018; Fernández-Götz and Roymans 2018), as well as the growing importance of theoretical perspectives influenced by postcolonial and decolonial approaches (cf. Belvedere and Bergemann 2021; Cahana-Blum and MacKendrick 2019; Gardner 2013), have opened up new methodological and theoretical avenues for studying the growing corpus of evidence. In this sense, the aims of this Element volume are manifold:

1) Move beyond the traditional focus on Roman frontier studies in order to concentrate on the actual moment of military conquest and its immediate aftermath.
2) Summarise a large body of recent archaeological data related to the Roman wars of conquest in the Late Republican and Early Imperial periods.
3) Contribute to the wider field of conflict archaeology through a number of theoretical and methodological reflections.

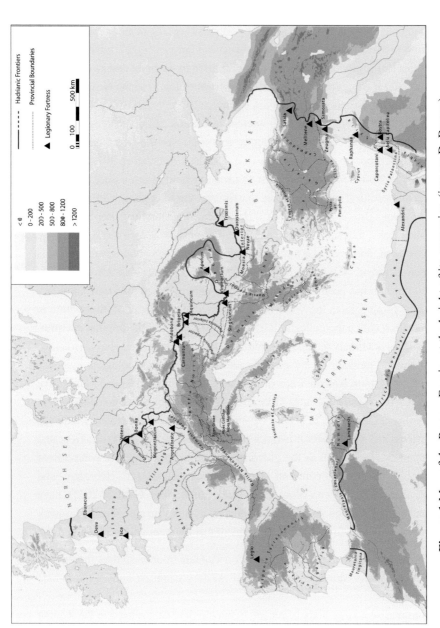

Figure 1 Map of the Roman Empire at the height of its expansion (image: D. Breeze)

4) Put the focus on the impact of the conquest on indigenous populations, thus reclaiming the memory of the communities that were forcibly incorporated into the Roman state.

In this Element, we use the term 'indigenous' primarily to refer to the Late Iron Age populations of Western and Central Europe that in many cases ended up being conquered by Rome, keeping in mind that indigenous groupings were dynamic and that there was considerable diversity between and within them. In this sense, our use of the term is very similar to the recent proposal by Shaw (in press). With this in mind, our goal is to present existing data in an accessible way and at the same time open new avenues for future research within and beyond the Roman world. To conform to the format of the Cambridge University Press Elements Series and their aim of producing concise overview works with a limit of around 30,000 words, we have decided to focus on a number of selected case studies. Geographically, our focus is on the Roman conquest of Western and Central Europe, with examples from ancient Gaul, Iberia, *Germania*, and Britain. Chronologically, we concentrate on the Late Republican and Early Imperial periods, more specifically on a number of military campaigns that range from the middle of the first century BC to the late first century AD. For reasons of space, we also focus primarily on the military campaigns and their repercussions, although we fully recognise the importance that other strategies of diplomacy and control (e.g. bribery of and collaboration with certain local elites) had in the process of integration into the Roman world. In any case, beyond this specific geographical and chronological scope, we hope that some of the approaches outlined in the volume can also be of interest to scholars working on other regions and periods.

After this introduction, the Element follows a roughly chronological order with most sections dedicated to a specific case study: Caesar's Gallic Wars (Section 2); the Cantabrian and Asturian Wars (Section 3); the Germanic Wars of Augustus (Section 4); and Rome's conquest of Britain (Section 5). Finally, Section 6 addresses some wider implications of the research for our understanding of Roman expansionism and its impact on local communities.

1.2 Beyond *Limes* Archaeology

Traditionally, much of the research on the Roman military has focused on so-called *limes* archaeology, i.e. the study of the frontier installations and infrastructure established in the provinces after the actual conquest had already taken place (Breeze 2018; Breeze et al. 2015; Schallmayer 2011). *Limes* archaeology represents a fascinating field of study that has made enormous contributions since the nineteenth century, not only from an academic perspective but also in terms of heritage management and visitor attractions through initiatives such as the Frontiers of the Roman Empire UNESCO World Heritage network. Monuments such as Hadrian's Wall and its associated forts in northern Britain, or the *Limes Germanicus* on the continent, are impressive examples of Rome's desire to consolidate its borders and regulate flow through them (Figure 2). However, due to its very nature, *limes* archaeology is mainly focused on the material remains that were aimed at protecting the conquered territories from potential outside attacks. Therefore, from this perspective the predominant approach has been to conceptualise the Roman army as the 'defender' of peace and civilian life in the provinces against external 'barbarian' enemies.

Our proposal in this Element volume is not necessarily in contradiction to *limes* archaeology, but it adopts a different, in our view complementary, approach, both temporally and conceptually. Our main focus is on the period of the Roman conquest itself, i.e. during the military campaigns as well as their immediate aftermath. This implies a different set of research questions and methodologies than *limes* archaeology. From the perspective of the archaeology of conquest, the Roman army acted as the aggressor, as a military force that imposed Roman rule on previously independent populations. Thus, the Roman military is frequently associated with episodes of violence and mass enslavement, and in some instances even potential cases of genocide. As previously indicated, this focus on the archaeology of

Figure 2 Image of Hadrian's Wall, which marked the northernmost frontier of the Roman Empire for nearly three centuries (photo: D. Breeze)

conquest is not in contradiction to *limes* archaeology, but it investigates a different side of the same coin. It does in any case highlight the 'darker sides' of Roman imperialism (Fernández-Götz et al. 2020; Raaflaub 2021; Taylor 2023), which means uncovering the more brutal sides and consequences of the conquest process.

1.3 Footprinting the Legions: Challenges and Possibilities

While most of the wars of conquest are mentioned – sometimes in considerable detail – in ancient written sources and the Roman army has been the focus of considerable scholarly work, for a long time the military campaigns themselves received relatively little attention from archaeologists. There are, of course, some exceptions of well-studied battlefields such as *Alesia* (Reddé and von Schnurbein 2001), but in general the amount of energy invested in the study of the archaeological remains of the conquest campaigns has been considerably less than in fields such as *limes* archaeology or the analysis of Roman domestic architecture, to name just two examples. At the risk of oversimplifying, and taking into account the existence of numerous nuances, we can identify three main factors that have played a role in this situation:

1) The problem of the chronological resolution of much of the archaeological material, which hinders analyses on the timescale of the *histoire événementielle* (at the level of specific decades or even years) and makes it difficult to establish direct connections to historically documented military campaigns. For example, based on material culture alone it is usually extremely difficult, if not impossible, to determine if a specific Gallic *oppidum* was abandoned shortly before, during, or slightly after Caesar's Gallic Wars.

2) The challenges in obtaining a tangible grasp on the remains of mobile armies and battlefields, a problem not exclusive to the archaeology of the Roman conquest but shared by much of conflict archaeology research. Marching camps, for example, were only occupied for a few days or weeks, usually leaving scarce material finds. Battlefields, for their part, are exceptional sites because of their large size (often covering hundreds of hectares), the absence of stratigraphy, the ephemeral nature of most material remains, and the scarcity of structural features. Battles can be very significant, but at the same time they very often last for only a few days or even hours. The immense damage and demographic losses inflicted by armies that ravaged the countryside using scorched-earth strategies are also normally difficult to identify archaeologically. Burning farmsteads, destroying harvests, stealing cattle, and enslaving, raping, or killing people are all acts that have an enormous impact on the civilian population (Figure 3), but can leave little or no trace in the archaeological record.

Figure 3 Destruction of a Germanic village by Roman troops during the Marcomannic Wars (AD 166–180); scene from the Column of Marcus Aurelius in Rome (image: © Alamy)

3) Finally, much of the research has traditionally tended to emphasise the supposedly 'positive' consequences of the Roman conquest, particularly in temperate Europe where integration into the Roman Empire has often been portrayed as the introduction of 'civilisation' to previously 'barbarian' populations. In this vein, the more brutal aspects of the conquest period have – consciously or unconsciously – frequently been ignored or under-played, with many narratives focusing on the supposed 'bright' sides, such as the spread of literacy, the development of villa landscapes, and the erection of monumental architecture. Partly for this reason, as well as the previous point about the scarcity and ephemeral nature of much of the conflict-related material evidence, scholarship has tended to focus more on remains that are easier to identify and more spectacular to preserve and present to the public: uncovering a mosaic or a Roman bath building has traditionally received more attention than trying to search for the tenuous traces of marching legions and destroyed hamlets. This, in a way, is not dissimilar to the tendency to prioritise the excavation of aristocratic villas or commander's headquarters instead of the homes of the humble peasants or the barracks of the ordinary soldiers.

The scarcity of direct material evidence for many of the military campaigns has led some scholars to conclude that the Roman wars of conquest had limited societal impact. For example, just a few decades ago Caesar's actions in northern Gaul or Augustus' conquest of northern Spain were almost untraceable in the archaeological record, which resulted in many ancient historians and archaeologists underestimating the dramatic consequences that the wars had on the indigenous communities of those regions – and this despite the ancient written sources explicitly mentioning the brutality of the campaigns.

However, as outlined at the beginning of this section, the situation has been changing in the last couple of decades. This is again due to several, sometimes interrelated, factors:

1) The increased quantity and quality of the archaeological data available for many regions, which have sparked a breakthrough in our knowledge of the military campaigns and their repercussions; the case studies presented in the following sections are a case in point.

2) The development of conflict archaeology, which has triggered interest in the topic of mass violence and led to an enhancement of the methodologies available for its study (Pollard and Banks 2005; Scott et al. 2009). The latter include specific research strategies for battle sites, the widespread use of remote sensing methods for identifying conflict-related military installations such as marching camps, and the use of isotope and ancient DNA analyses for the study of human remains (cf. Roymans and Fernández-Götz 2018).

3) The influence of postcolonial and decolonial thinking, which has generated greater interest in the negative consequences of imperialism and conquest, including in the case of the Roman world (e.g. Lavan 2020; Mattingly 2011; Padilla Peralta 2020). In addition, and partly complementary to this, there is growing interest within archaeology for perspectives 'from below' centred on the lives of ordinary people (Thurston and Fernández-Götz 2021), and Roman studies are also increasingly engaging with this trend (Bowes 2021).

1.4 Themes and Methodologies of an Archaeology of the Roman Conquest

The maturity of conflict archaeology has led to the recognition that this sub-discipline is about much more than just the study of battlefields (Fernández-Götz and Roymans 2018; Saunders 2012). While the latter continues to be very important and attracts the greatest attention, there are many other ways in which archaeology can, directly or indirectly, contribute to the study of the Roman wars of conquest and their social impact on affected communities (Roymans and Fernández-Götz 2019). This includes, for instance, the investigation of military encampments from the war and post-war periods; the study of the weaponry and fortification techniques employed by the different combating parties; the analysis of indigenous settlement patterns to identify potential cases of discontinuity; the use of palaeoenvironmental data to assess the impact of

Roman expansion on the landscape; and the research of post-conflict ritual depositions and/or commemorative structures. While there are multiple avenues for research, here we want to highlight the potential of archaeology for our understanding of the Roman conquest in regard to three main themes, which will be illustrated in more detail in the following sections:

1) *Roman military installations and infrastructure.* The starting point for archaeological research is usually the identification and exploration of Roman military structures (both permanent forts and temporary camps) and marching routes. This type of research is not new in itself and has been pursued since antiquarian times. The main difference is that we now have at our disposal a set of advanced methods that is revolutionising our knowledge. This includes, for example, the systematic use of aerial photography and LiDAR data, which has led to the identification of large numbers of previously unknown marching camps, particularly in mountainous and/or forested areas such as northern Spain (Section 3). Once identified, the study of Roman military installations is benefiting from enhanced excavation and documentation methods, as well as metal-detecting and geophysical surveys. An example of this type of state-of-the-art investigation is the work carried out at the Caesarian site of Hermeskeil in the Trier region of Germany (Hornung 2018).

2) *Battlefields and sieges.* Directly linked to the previous point is the identification and study of battlefields and sieges related to the Roman conquest. Some of them are mentioned in written sources and have been identified archaeologically without any reservation, as in the case of *Alesia* in central Gaul (Reddé 2018a; Reddé and von Schnurbein 2001). Other identifications are still debated, such as the Battle of the Teutoburg Forest at the site of Kalkriese in Lower Saxony (Burmeister 2022; Moosbauer 2009; Wells 2003), or just tentative as in the case of *Bergida* – Monte Bernorio in northern Spain (Brown et al. 2017). Finally, there are also battles not mentioned in ancient written sources (or at least not in sources that have survived) but which have been identified archaeologically, such as Harzhorn in Lower Saxony (Meyer 2018; Moosbauer 2018). Building upon the seminal work undertaken by Scott and his team on the nineteenth-century Battle of Little Bighorn in the USA (Scott et al. 1989), in the past few decades archaeology has made substantial progress in developing fieldwork strategies adapted to the special characteristics of battle sites (Meller 2009; Scott and McFeaters 2011). Most effective appears to be a combination of survey techniques (metal detection, aerial photography, LiDAR-based elevation models, etc.) and small-scale targeted excavations aimed at testing hypotheses. This methodology has been

successfully applied, for example, at the Second Punic War Battle of *Baecula* in southeast Spain (Bellón et al. 2015). In addition to open battles, such as Kalkriese and Harzhorn, attacks on fortified indigenous settlements by the Roman army are also attested. Evidence for the latter can sometimes be uncovered on a spectacular scale, as demonstrated by the thousands of arrowheads identified at the *oppidum* of La Loma in northern Spain (Peralta et al. 2022; cf. Section 3) or the hundreds of lead sling bullets found at Burnswark hillfort in Scotland (Reid and Nicholson 2019; cf. Section 5). These types of finds, together with other characteristic items such as the hobnails from the sandal-boots (*caligae*) of the Roman soldiers, help us to 'footprint' the legions during the conquest campaigns.

3) *Demographic consequences of the conquest.* Written accounts from the classical world as well as analogies with later historical periods clearly show that military campaigns can have a dramatic, negative effect on the demography of conquered regions. This refers not only to the casualties produced by direct military combat, but also to massacres of non-combatant populations, the effects of systematic scorched-earth campaigns by invading armies (leading to hunger, starvation, and illness), the deportation and mass enslavement of groups, and the fleeing of refugees (Figure 4). Mass violence appears to have been a systematic aspect of Rome's military expansion and

Figure 4 Refugees from the battle of *Baecula* (Proyecto Baecula/PastWomen; illustration: I. Diéguez)

Roman society was very familiar with the use of collective violence, sometimes in extreme forms. This is amply illustrated in Roman iconography, for example on Trajan's Column and the Column of Marcus Aurelius. In some cases, classical authors report estimated numbers of casualties: for example, Appian (*Roman History* 4. *The Celtic Book* 1) and Plutarch (*Caesar* 15) claim that Caesar killed one million and enslaved another million of his Gallic opponents. Even if these numbers were exaggerated, there is little doubt that the conquest of Gaul must have had a substantial demographic impact. However, historical sources also suggest that there were major regional differences in the direct demographic effect of the Roman wars of conquest. Whereas in some regions the population seems to have remained fairly stable, in others the annexation process was extremely violent and would have led to a significant demographic decline, with episodes of at least partial depopulation in the years or even decades following the conquest (cf Section 2.5). Archaeology can make a significant contribution to this debate by studying settlement pattern trajectories in case study regions: do we observe a marked continuity between the pre- and post-conquest periods, or rather a sharp discontinuity that could reflect a demographic decrease caused by the conquest? A precondition for this assessment is the availability of a substantial body of high-quality settlement data in combination with a well-developed chronological framework. In addition, palaeoenvironmental data in the form of pollen diagrams can shed light on human landscape use that might contribute to the discussion: was there an increase in cultivated areas, or rather a reduction of human activity and a surge in arboreal pollen?

1.5 Towards Interdisciplinary and Multidimensional Approaches

The study of the Roman conquest and its consequences requires interdisciplinary and multidimensional approaches. Interdisciplinary, because it should combine all available sources of information by incorporating both literary accounts and archaeological data within a contextual framework. Thus, classical authors often provide crucial information when describing aspects such as military routes, siege works, and battles, as well as elements of the wider background including information on political strategies, alliances, and negotiations. At the same time, each individual source needs to be subjected to a critical and contextual analysis in order to assess its degree of reliability, disentangling aspects such as literary *topoi*, personal agendas, and imperial propaganda. When referring to outside enemies and conquered populations, we always need to keep in mind that classical sources are providing etic descriptions that are often incomplete and influenced by biases, stereotypes, and political agendas (Woolf 2011).

Archaeological sources, for their part, also require contextual analyses that take into account the nature of the evidence, including issues of visibility of the archaeological record. For example, it is well known that battlefields were subject to post-battle looting and cleaning activities in the hours and days following the events, which heavily shaped the record that archaeologists can identify (cf. Ball 2014 for Roman battlefields). Similarly, the scarcity of human remains at most conflict sites can largely be explained by the post-combat activities that would have taken place there. These could include, among others, the dumping of bodies into mass graves or the cremation of corpses without placing the remains in archaeologically identifiable formal burials.

In this Element volume, we also argue for the use of a multidimensional approach in order to understand the process of Roman conquest (including 'failed' attempts, such as in *Germania Magna* and northern Britain, see Sections 4 and 5). Our model distinguishes between a time-space, a cultural, and an institutional dimension (Figure 5). Regarding the time-space dimension, archaeologists engaged in fieldwork related to the Roman conquest invest considerable energy in local research, therefore focusing on the study of the micro-scale and usually also the short-term. While this is necessary and understandable, short-term processes on a micro-scale can only be fully comprehended within a broader temporal and macro-regional context. Similarly, all wars have a 'hard core'

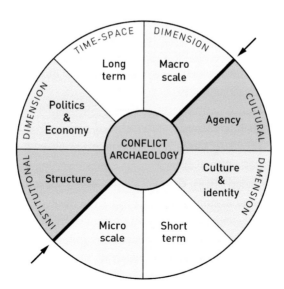

Figure 5 Model of a multidimensional approach to the study of past conflict, using an historical–anthropological perspective (authors, inspired by Slofstra 2002)

institutional dimension that requires consideration of the role of power relations, social structures, and the close links with the economic domain. But historical and social sciences have also demonstrated that conflicts cannot be properly understood without paying attention to the cultural dimension, where we are confronted with the impact of ideologies, belief systems, identity constructions, and ritual. At the same time, we need to allocate sufficient space to the human agency of both individuals and groups. The dialectics between agency and structure, short-term events versus longer-term processes, need to be considered in order to grasp the complexity of the phenomenon. From the above, it follows that approaches need to be multi-scalar, both in a geographical and chronological sense: from the local to the regional and supra-regional, from the individual to the collective, and from the immediate event to the wider social, political, and economic contexts of a given period, including precedents and aftermath.

1.6 Roman Expansionism as the Product of a Predatory Regime

The final point that we want to address in this introductory section is the nature of Roman expansionism. This has been a matter of intense scholarly debate, and we need to acknowledge the heterogeneity of strategies and approaches that existed over time and space. However, from a macro-perspective we conceptualise the Late Republican and Early Imperial Roman political economy as a 'predatory regime' (see Fernández-Götz et al. 2020 for a more in-depth discussion). Our use of the term is based on González-Ruibal (2015: 424) who, following Mbembe (2001), describes predatory regimes as being 'characterised by the militarization of power and trade, pillage as an economic strategy, the pursuit of private interest under public command and the conversion of brute violence into legitimate authority'.

The Late Republican period was marked by considerable social and political violence, both internalised in the form of various Roman Civil Wars (Lange and Vervaet 2019; Maschek 2018) and externalised through the conquest of new territories (Badian 1968), sometimes resorting to extreme forms of violence (Barrandon 2018). Caesar's Gallic Wars (Section 2) are a case in point, but many other examples also existed. Even during the long period of the so-called *Pax Romana* (a term that is itself rather misleading), aggressive military campaigns continued to be a defining feature of Roman imperial policies, from the Germanic Wars (Section 4) to the conquests of Britain (Section 5) and *Dacia*, or the brutal suppression of the Jewish revolts (Figure 6).

The process of annexation and exploitation of new territories by Rome can often be characterised as pillage carried out in order to increase the personal

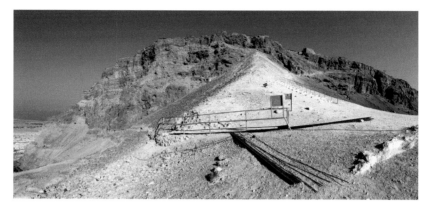

Figure 6 The Jewish stronghold of Masada, with Roman assault ramp in the foreground (photo: M. Fernández-Götz)

wealth and prestige of certain individuals and elite factions. Caesar's enormous personal enrichment through the Gallic Wars is a prime example (cf. Section 2.6), but other Roman leaders also resorted to aggressive military campaigns in order to increase their personal prestige and obtain revenues through the plundering and subsequent exploitation of foreign lands. Within this model, state gain was often just a secondary outcome of individual and familial agendas that employed warfare and the extraction of external resources (both human, i.e. slaves, and non-human, e.g. precious metals or grain) as a way of attaining or consolidating their privileged positions at the top of Roman society. These asymmetric power dynamics and the 'dark sides' of the conquest process need to be highlighted if we want to construct more comprehensive and inclusive approaches that take into account the suffering inflicted on millions of people, including episodes of large-scale killing, displacement, and disorientation (Fernández-Götz et al. 2020; Padilla Peralta 2020; Shaw in press).

Having said this, it should be noted that the predatory regime was not equally intense in all the regions conquered by Rome, nor over the entire duration of the Roman state. The model of aggressive military conquest and large-scale plundering applies to certain territories such as large parts of Gaul, Iberia, and *Dacia*, but not necessarily to other regions like *Noricum*, *Cyrenaica*, and Cappadocia. We also need to keep in mind that indigenous societies were not homogenous blocks: some communities, factions, or individuals were actually allied to the Romans, as observed for example during the Gallic Wars, when some *civitates* loyal to Rome benefited from the conquest process to the detriment of neighbouring communities. Power dynamics were often fluid and dynamic, with changes occurring through time and space, sometimes even within short periods of time. Neither 'Romans' nor 'natives' were homogeneous groups, and collaboration and hybridisation took place alongside resistance and repression. Moreover, while the use of binary terms like conqueror/conquered, Roman/indigenous, or domination/resistance can make sense when analysing many scenarios of military conquest and the situation in the periods immediately afterwards, those terms very often lose their significance as time passes. Grasping the complexity of existing situations is fundamental when analysing the process of integration of communities into the Roman state.

2 Caesar's Invasion: The Conquest of *Gallia Comata*

2.1 Gaul on the Eve of Caesar's Conquest

Caesar's accounts of his Gallic Wars (58–51 BC) form a unique document for the study of Rome's military expansion since they were written by the leading general himself. Although elements of personal propaganda and the rhetoric of an imperial ideology infuse his commentaries, they represent one of the most detailed accounts of the Roman wars of conquest (cf. Kraus 2009; Raaflaub 2017; Riggsby 2006). The archaeology of the Gallic campaigns, for its part, has experienced a significant surge in recent decades, with many new discoveries and the introduction of novel theoretical and methodological approaches (Roymans and Fernández-Götz 2023). This section presents an overview of the materiality of the Gallic Wars (Figure 7), showing how archaeology can contribute to a better understanding of the process of conquest and its impact on the conquered societies.

Caesar's conquest should be placed within the context of the long-term history of Rome's economic and military expansion in the Gallic periphery. Initially, Roman interests were primarily focused on the Mediterranean part of Gaul, where the Greek colony of *Massalia* traditionally held a dominant position. The first step towards territorial expansion was the conquest of southern Gaul (*Gallia Transalpina*) in the 120s BC, followed by the establishment of a formal provincial organisation, which included confiscations of land for Roman citizens and the foundation of the Roman colony of *Narbo Martius* (Luley 2020).

The conquest of *Gallia Transalpina* brought the peoples of interior Gaul into the direct sphere of Roman influence. Independent Gaul, referred to as *Gallia Comata*, experienced a spectacular increase in long-distance trade with Roman Italy. Roman merchants further intensified their lucrative trade based on the large-scale export of Italian wine (Poux 2004) in exchange for Gallic slaves. Rome also established formal political alliances with certain Gallic groups. The *Aedui* already had a special clientship treaty with Rome from the mid-second century BC on, which brought them the title *fratres et consanguinei* of the Roman people.

Figure 7 Location of the main sites mentioned in Section 2 (authors)

At the beginning of Caesar's campaigns, there were around sixty recorded tribal polities (*civitates*) within *Gallia Comata*, roughly the area bounded by the Rhine, the Atlantic, and the Pyrenees (Fichtl 2012) (Figure 8). *Gallia Comata*, however, did not constitute a homogeneous political or cultural entity, nor did its inhabitants share a notion of collective ethnic identity. Caesar described three major subgroupings: the *Belgae* in the North, the *Aquitani* in the southwest, and the *Celtae* in the centre, stating that they differed in language, institutions, and laws (*BG* 1.1). Archaeological evidence shows that there was considerable sociopolitical and economic diversity across Gaul (Brun and Ruby 2008; Fernández-Götz 2014; Ralston 2019). Most striking is the distinction between a zone of 'tribal states' with urbanised *oppida* in central and eastern Gaul, versus a zone on the northern fringe inhabited by Germanic peoples with a highly decentralised settlement system and less marked social hierarchies that were heavily based on 'power from below' mechanisms.

2.2 Strategies and Motivations of a Colonial War

Caesar's Gallic Wars can best be characterised as a 'colonial war' (Woolf 2019). The conquest started in 58 BC and it took eight years of campaigning with an army of seven to ten legions plus auxiliary troops. The army resided in marching

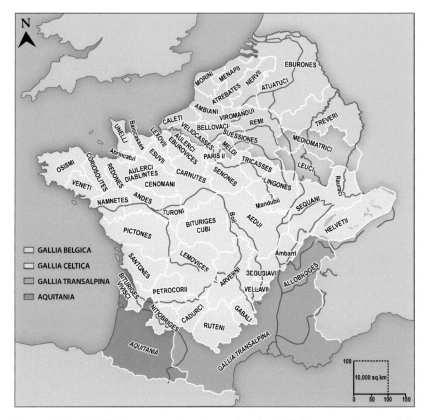

Figure 8 Gaul: Tribal groups and major regional subdivisions on the eve of the
Gallic Wars (after Ralston 2019, modified by authors)

camps during the campaigning season and settled – for logistical reasons and to
control recently conquered areas – in quarters throughout the winter months. As
with most colonial wars, conflict was highly asymmetrical. The Roman army
was overwhelmingly superior to the Gallic armies confronting them in terms of
discipline, equipment, logistics, and technical skills. Brutal violence against
peoples that resisted domination was a standard feature of the Roman strategy.
Caesar's narrative informs us about various forms of large-scale violence,
including the looting and destruction of indigenous settlements, mass enslavement, massacres, and even cases of genocide. This use of brutal violence, in
combination with occasional clemency employed as part of the political strategy, is described in detail in his *Commentarii* (Barrandon 2018; Raaflaub 2021;
Taylor 2023).

While the Roman invasion was resisted by most tribal polities, others were
allied to Caesar and benefited from the conquest, for example seeing an increase

in their territories at the cost of their neighbours. Additionally, the complexity and fluidity of existing scenarios must also be considered. Thus, pro- and anti-Roman factions could exist within the same *civitas*, and sometimes even the same family, and some groups changed sides during the course of the war. Both literary sources and the continuously growing amount of archaeological evidence highlight the diversity present in Gallic communities before, during, and after the Roman conquest (Fernández-Götz 2014; Fichtl 2012).

Caesar's commentaries hardly inform us about the motivations behind his Gallic campaigns. Although he was clearly the aggressor, he often used a defensive rhetoric, referring to the duty to protect Rome's allies to justify his campaigns. However, his wars should primarily be understood against the background of the fierce competition for power in Late Republican Rome. The Gallic Wars provided him military prestige, power, and personal wealth that could be invested in realising his political ambitions in Rome (Woolf 2019). The economic dimension of his Gallic campaigns remains heavily underexposed in his writings, but Suetonius (*Jul.* 25–26, 28, 38, 54) frequently refers to the amazing wealth accumulated by the general in Gaul in the form of tribute levies, booty, ransoms, and by the selling of slaves. Caesar started his Gallic campaigns as a debtor, but ended them as one of the richest magnates of the Roman Republic.

2.3 The Materiality of the Roman Conquest in Central and Eastern Gaul

Archaeology has been able to contribute to the study of the Roman conquest of Gaul in multiple ways. The search for archaeological remains began to attract significant interest after the mid-nineteenth century, receiving its initial push from the support given by the French Emperor Napoleon III, who was fascinated by Caesar's account. He provided resources for work at sites named in the commentaries, most notably *Alesia*, *Gergovia*, and *Uxellodunum*. This research was closely connected to the political atmosphere of the time, illustrating the general rise of nationalism in Europe and the use of the past for modern political purposes. In France, this was closely linked to the cultivation of collective memory and identity (Dietler 1994), as expressed in the erection in 1865 of a monumental statue of the Gallic leader Vercingetorix at the site of the *oppidum* of *Alesia* (Figure 9), where Caesar had defeated the confederated Gallic army in 52 BC.

The excavations undertaken at *Alesia* from 1861 to 1865 uncovered ample material evidence for the siege and battle described by Caesar (*BG* 7.68–89). Among the discoveries were a variety of weaponry, the remains of the siege-works (which Napoleon III named 'contravallation' – facing the *oppidum* – and

Figure 9 Statue of Vercingetorix at *Alesia*, erected in 1865 (photo: Myrabella, CC BY-SA 4.0)

'circumvallation' – facing outwards), and a number of supposed Roman camps (*castra*) as well as some smaller *castella* in the intervening gaps. Between 1991 and 1997 new archaeological research was undertaken at *Alesia* within the framework of a joint Franco-German project (Reddé 2018a; Reddé and von Schnurbein 2001). These investigations only confirmed the locations of three of the Roman camps that the nineteenth century excavations had claimed to discover: firstly, Camp C to the north on Bussy Hill; secondly, Camp B to the south of the siege works, the largest of all the known camps, which might have been that of Caesar himself; and thirdly, the nearby and smaller Camp A. The remaining camps that were identified under the patronage of Napoleon III are more doubtful and cannot be attributed with any certainty to the time of the siege. Finally, there are some military installations that were either confirmed or newly discovered during the investigations carried out in the 1990s, for example a possible, but now highly eroded, camp on Mont Réa, as well as *castellum* 11 in the southern sector, and a previously unknown *castellum* at Fortin de l'Épineuse (Figure 10).

In general terms, there is a noteworthy discrepancy between the number of confirmed archaeological structures identified at *Alesia* and what could be expected for a Roman army of between 40,000 and 60,000 men plus auxiliary

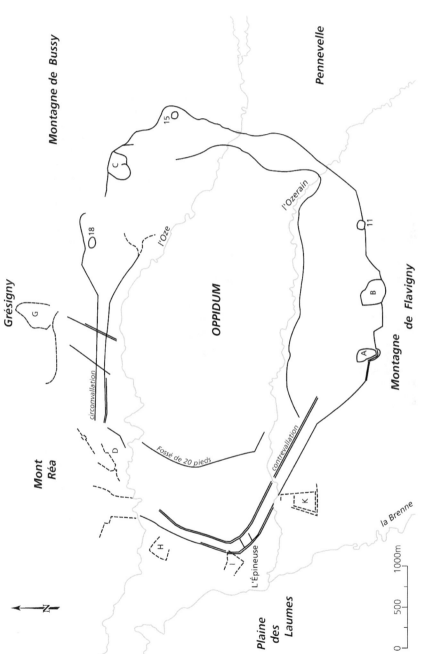

Figure 10 Topographical sketch map of the siege of *Alesia* (after Redde 2018a)

troops (Reddé 2018a). However, this is not surprising given the rather ephemeral nature of most of the installations, and the impact of post-battle activities and post-depositional processes, which generally affect the preservation of battlefield remains. The effect of these factors in the preservation and visibility of battlefield remains has been amply attested for both ancient and modern case studies (Roymans and Fernández-Götz 2018; Scott and McFeaters 2011).

While *Alesia* is without doubt the most important and best investigated battlefield in Gaul, other sites and types of evidence also deserve attention. In general terms, fieldwork projects across the territories of ancient Gaul are continually providing new insights, sometimes confirming, and other times nuancing or revising earlier interpretations (Fitzpatrick and Haselgrove 2019; Reddé 2018b). For example, the *oppidum* of Puy d'Issolud has been confirmed as the site of *Uxellodunum*, where the last major siege and battle of the Gallic Wars took place in 51 BC. The archaeological investigations at Puy d'Issolud provided a great number of artefacts, including numerous arrowheads that testify to the attack suffered by the besieged Gauls when they tried to collect water from a spring below the *oppidum* (Girault 2013).

Other instances where archaeological work has provided insights into key scenarios of the Gallic Wars include the Roman military camp at Mauchamp, which is likely related to the battle of the Aisne against the *Belgae* in 57 BC, and the famous Siege of *Gergovia* in 52 BC (Reddé 2019). While these two sites have a long history of research, there have also been some completely unexpected discoveries made since the start of the twenty-first century. An example is the identification of a Caesarian military camp at Hermeskeil, located in the immediate vicinity of the Treveran *oppidum* of Otzenhausen (Hornung 2018) (Figure 11). The absence of timber and stone structures in the interior suggests that the soldiers were accommodated in tents, probably in the context of the campaigns of Caesar's lieutenant Labienus against the *Treveri*.

It is much more difficult to identify Gallic *oppida* that were used by the Roman army as winter quarters, control stations, or supply centres. A notable exception is the Treveran *oppidum* of the Titelberg (Luxemburg). Recent excavations uncovered the remains of a large building complex interpreted as a Roman trading post that was already in use in the pre-conquest period, while numerous Roman *militaria* point to a Roman military presence during the conquest and the early post-conquest period (Metzler et al. 2018).

A basic precondition for getting a grip on the materiality of the Gallic conquest is the availability of an adequate typo-chronological framework of Roman *militaria*. In the last two decades important progress has been made in this regard (Poux 2008; Reddé 2018b). Interestingly, iron hobnails from sandal-boots (*caligae*) appear to be key objects for tracing the 'footprints' of Roman soldiers.

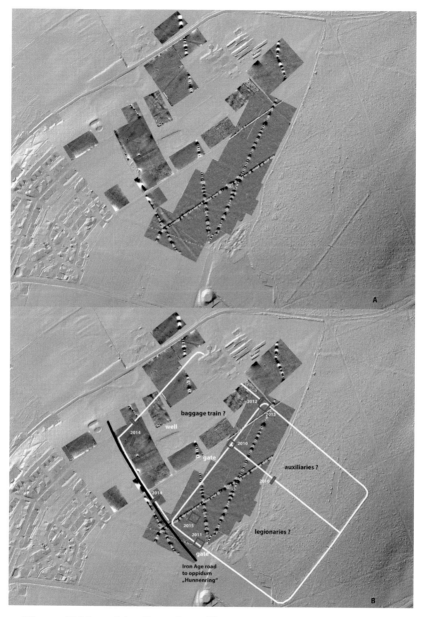

Figure 11 Map of the Caesarian military camp at Hermeskeil. Outlined in red are the excavation trenches opened between 2010 and 2015 (after Hornung 2018)

2.4 Genocide in the Far North?

In the northernmost regions of Gaul, archaeological research from the past two decades has substantially changed our knowledge of the Roman conquest and its immediate aftermath. Until recently, the Caesarian conquest was almost completely intangible in the archaeological record of the Lower Rhine/Meuse region. However, the scarcity of archaeological evidence does not mean that the societies on the northern periphery did not suffer serious consequences as a result of the Roman presence there. According to the writings of Caesar, the 'Germanic' frontier zone was likely the area of Gaul most dramatically affected by the conquest (Roymans 2019a; Roymans and Fernández-Götz 2023). In these regions, we observe episodes of destruction, mass enslavement, deportation, and sometimes even genocide or ethnocide of resistant groups.

One of the 'crime scenes' of the Gallic Wars identified over the last decade and a half is the fortification of Thuin (Belgium), which has been interpreted as the *oppidum* of the *Aduatuci* that was besieged and conquered by the Roman army in 57 BC. According to Caesar (*BG* 2.29–35), the *Aduatuci* had assembled there, but after the Roman victory, the entire population of 53,000 individuals was sold as slaves and deported to Italy, in what might be classified as a case of ethnocide (i.e. the destruction of a group's culture and identity without the massacre of its people; cf. Chalk and Jonassohn 1990).

The reasons for identifying the fortification of Thuin, which occupies a plateau of more than 13 ha, as the *oppidum* of the *Aduatuci* can be summarised as follows (Roymans and Scheers 2012):

1) The location of the site in the territory that written sources attribute to the *Aduatuci*.
2) The topographical similarities with the description provided by Caesar.
3) The discovery of several Gallo-Belgic gold coin hoards, dated to the early 50s BC and seemingly reflective of a single event.
4) The almost total absence of Roman coins within the site, meaning that the fortification had lost its central function in the post-conquest period.
5) Finally, evidence for an attack on the fortification by the Roman army, as indicated by several concentrations of Roman lead sling bullets (Figure 12).

Following their defeat, the *Aduatuci* no longer played any politically significant role, to the degree that they shortly thereafter disappeared from the Gallic tribal map.

The identification of Thuin as the *oppidum* of the *Aduatuci* attacked by Caesar has led to new archaeological fieldwork. Small-scale excavations and surveys inside the fortification produced a complete Late Iron Age sword, mid-first century BC gold coins, and a new series of Roman lead sling bullets (Paridaens 2020). The new evidence collected so far further strengthens the argument for the identification of the site as the *oppidum* of the *Aduatuci*. Geochemical analyses carried out on the sling bullets indicate that the lead

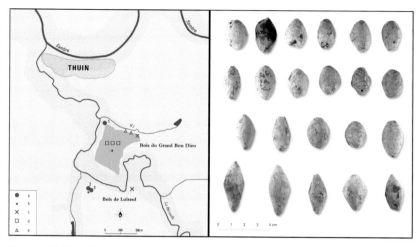

Figure 12 Late Iron Age fortification at Thuin. Left: topography including the location of various finds categories. a) gold hoards; b) isolated gold coin(s); c) concentration of Roman sling bullets; d) iron tools; e) bronze ornaments and appliques. Right: Roman lead sling bullets (after Roymans and Scheers 2012)

originated from mines in southeast Spain (Paridaens et al. 2020). This fits well with the information that Caesar's army included specialised units of slingers from the Balearic Islands (*BG* 2.7), who may have used lead that they brought from Iberia. The portable finds from within the fortification can be dated to La Tène D2, and the coin spectrum helps to narrow down the chronology even further, as it consists almost exclusively of mid-first century BC gold staters.

Another 'crime scene' can probably be related to Caesar's massacre of the Germanic *Tencteri* and *Usipetes* in 55 BC (Roymans 2018, 2019a). Both tribes had migrated from inner *Germania*, where they had given up their homelands due to the pressure of the *Suebi* (*BG* 4.4–15). In the winter of 56/55 BC, they crossed the Lower Rhine and sent messengers asking Caesar for permission to settle in Gaul, a request that was rejected. The Germans gathered with all their possessions in an encampment which included men, women, and children. Caesar attacked the camp and ordered his troops to kill as many as possible, including women and children. The fleeing Germans were finally trapped at the nearby confluence of the rivers Rhine and Meuse, where they were slaughtered in great numbers.

The location of the massacre has been identified as the site of Kessel-Lith in the Dutch river area, where a large number of Late Iron Age finds, as well as numerous human remains, have been recovered over the years during large-scale dredging operations in an ancient bed of the Meuse (Roymans 2018).

Initially interpreted as the result of votive deposits, a reassessment of the archaeological evidence and the results of recent radiocarbon and isotope analyses make it more plausible to connect a significant portion of the finds with a battle-related event. The likelihood of this interpretation derives from a combination of historical, palaeogeographical, and archaeological data:

1) The palaeogeographical reconstruction of the area around Kessel-Lith is consistent with the topography for the location of the massacre as described by Caesar.

2) The historical date of the event in the mid-first century BC falls within the date range of the recovered archaeological materials (including a series of La Tène D2 swords).

3) The large number of human skeletal remains, including bones of women, children, and elderly individuals, fits well with the anthropological profile that we can expect from Caesar's account (Figure 13). Moreover, some of the bones show traces of weapon injuries.

4) The dispersal of human bones in the ancient riverbed in a zone extending some 3 km suggests a link to a major battle rather than a cult place.

5) The radiocarbon dating of human bones indicates a solid clustering in the Late Iron Age.

6) Several isotope analyses of dental remains point to a non-local origin for the dead.

Figure 13 Human remains from the battle-related find complex dredged from the River Meuse at Kessel-Lith (after Roymans 2004)

If we accept the direct link with the battle of 55 BC against the *Tencteri* and *Usipetes*, then Kessel-Lith represents an archaeological site where we are directly confronted with evidence of a Roman massacre during the process of imperial expansion. Adopting a comparative, cross-cultural perspective, Caesar's actions against the two tribes can probably be classified as a genocidal act (Taylor 2023). The same qualification can be used for his efforts to destroy the *Eburones* as a tribal group: the campaigns were meant to annihilate this group and its name (*stirps ac nomen civitatis tollatur*, cf. *BG* 6.34.8). Genocide is generally defined as a practice involving the mass killing of a national, ethnic, or religious group in combination with the intent to annihilate that group (Bloxham and Moses 2010). While some scholars have argued that it is anachronistic to use this term for mass killings in pre-modern periods, others have employed it as a historical concept for cross-cultural comparative studies from antiquity onwards (Chalk and Jonassohn 1990; Kiernan 2007; Kiernan et al. 2023; Van Wees 2010).

Several explanations, partly interrelated, can be given for the extremely violent behaviour of the Roman army in this northernmost area of Gaul. Firstly, the scarcity of major defended *oppida* (Fernández-Götz 2014; Roymans 1990), which Caesar could have used as military targets. Secondly, the less hierarchical social organisation of these northern societies, which lacked powerful aristocracies that could be targeted by Roman diplomacy; tribal leaders, like the Eburonean kings Ambiorix and Catuvolcus, highly depended on 'power from below' mechanisms (Thurston and Fernández-Götz 2021), in particular tribal councils. Useful here is the model of heterarchical societies with a high degree of collective control of leadership positions (Hill 2006). In situations of crisis, charismatic war leaders could raise and command large armies, but their power position was usually of a temporary nature. Finally, the extremely negative ethnic stereotyping of the northern peoples by Rome as *Germani* – synonymous with 'barbarians' *par excellence* – seems to have lowered the threshold for annihilating resistant groups (Roymans 2019a).

2.5 The Demographic Impact of the Conquest

There is little doubt that many Gallic communities were dramatically affected by the Caesarian conquest. As mentioned in Section 1, even if the numbers of casualties and enslaved people provided by Appian (*Roman History* 4. *The Celtic Book* 1) and Plutarch (*Caesar* 15) were exaggerated, the impact of the military campaigns on the demography of the overall population must have been substantial (see also Reddé 2022). Archaeology has the potential to assess the demographic consequences of the conquest through the study of regional settlement patterns (Roymans 2019a). Written sources suggest that the demographic impact experienced by Gallic societies during and immediately after the conquest had major regional variations. While in some areas the population seems to have remained relatively stable, in other regions the extremely violent process of conquest resulted in major disruptions. The latter scenario seems to apply to many tribal groups in the 'Germanic' frontier zone, which were subjected to a scorched-earth strategy, in particular the *Menapii*, *Morini*, and *Eburones*. The Roman strategy consisted of large-scale razing of settlements by fire, taking prisoners, carrying off cattle, and destroying harvests.

The interpretation of Caesar's narrative is, however, not free of controversies. Although it is clear that both the *Eburones* and the *Aduatuci* did not survive the conquest period as tribal groups, there are differing opinions among ancient historians about the veracity of Caesar's assertions. Some scholars take his account of the destruction of the aforementioned tribes quite literally, whereas others see it as a rhetorical act of political propaganda (Heinrichs 2008). While their absence from the political map after the conquest was not necessarily due to complete destruction, it seems likely that at least some of the tribal groups in the far north of Gaul experienced a substantial population decrease. In this context, we should also take into account the radically altered tribal map of the Lower Germanic frontier in the early post-conquest period, combined with reports of the substantial settlement of immigrant groups from the east bank of the Rhine. This settlement of new groups – the *Batavi* are even said to have moved to uninhabited land (*vacua cultoribus*) in the Dutch river area (Tac. *Hist.* 4.12) – suggests a period of demographic decline in the preceding years.

The systematic study of settlement evidence offers possibilities for testing the historical model of significant settlement discontinuity in some regions based on Caesar's accounts. If we assume that his activities led to a substantial decline in population, the most practical method is to investigate regional habitation trends for the first century BC, with particular attention paid to possible discontinuities (Roymans 2019a).

The evidence of (partially) excavated settlements from five well-explored test regions allows some preliminary conclusions to be drawn about the demographic impact of the Caesarian conquest (Figure 14). In the far north of Gaul, a decentralised settlement pattern, consisting of small sites of only a few contemporary farmhouses, was typical. In general, the first century BC appears to have been a period of substantial settlement abandonment and demographic decrease. Although complete depopulation is not observed (with perhaps the exception of region 1), all the case studies show a more or less pronounced discontinuity between La Tène D1 and the Early Roman period (Roymans 2019a).

The repopulation patterns in the different regions are also interesting to analyse (Table 1). In the Dutch east river area, new settlements were formed beginning in the period between 50 and 20 BC, whereas in the Meuse/Demer/

Table 1 Degree of settlement discontinuity in five test regions in the extreme
north of Gaul (after Roymans 2019a)

Region	Degree of discontinuity	Dating	Recolonisation
South Holland	total(?) discontinuity	1st century BC	Claudian
Meuse/Demer/ Scheldt area	substantial discontinuity	1st century BC	Augustan
Dutch east river area	partial discontinuity	mid-1st century BC	50–20 BC
Cologne hinterland	substantial discontinuity	1st century BC	Claudian
Hesbaye/Tongeren region	substantial discontinuity	1st century BC	Augustan

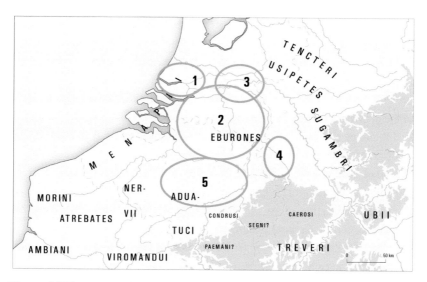

Figure 14 Five test regions with good settlement evidence for the investigation
of demographic trends during the Late Iron Age and Early Roman period. 1.
South Holland; 2. Meuse/Demer/Scheldt region; 3. Dutch East River area; 4.
Cologne hinterland; 5. Tongeren area (after Roymans 2019a)

Scheldt region and probably also the Hesbaye area, this took place a generation
later, in the Augustan period. The most dramatic depopulation was seen in
South Holland and the Cologne hinterland, where recolonisation is only observable in the Claudian period.

To what extent can the evidence for a substantial demographic regression in the first century BC be explained by Caesar's destructive practices? In this region, a link with Caesar's campaigns is plausible, although no hard proof is available because the abandonment of settlements generally cannot be dated to a specific year or decade. Other factors (famine, environmental problems) may also have played a role in the abandonment of certain sites, but in general terms the Roman conquest seems to have been the major explanation.

2.6 Rome's Hunger for Gold: The Testimony of Coinage

Another topic that we would like to address is the extraction of mobile wealth from Gallic groups by Caesar. There is abundant written evidence that the systematic plundering of precious metals was a key strategy of Roman warfare during the Late Republic (Badian 1968; Raaflaub 2021; Roymans 1990). Caesar's war narrative is silent about this issue, but important information comes from his later biographer Suetonius, who blamed him for the large-scale plunder of Gallic *oppida* and sanctuaries and of having enriched himself enormously with wealth stored there, most notably in the form of gold: 'In Gaul he pillaged shrines and temples of the gods filled with offerings, and oftener sacked towns for the sake of plunder than for any fault. In consequence he had more gold than he knew what to do with, and offered it for sale throughout Italy and the provinces at the rate of three thousand sesterces the pound' (Suetonius *Jul.* 54). Since the usual price of gold was 4,000 sesterces, it is evident that Caesar greatly inflated the Italian gold market.

To what extent is this drain of mobile wealth during the Gallic Wars archaeologically tangible? The testimony of precious metal coinage can offer some interesting clues. At the time of the conquest parts of central and eastern *Gallia Comata* belonged to the '*zone du denier*', which was aligned on the Roman denarius. However, Belgic Gaul belonged to the zone that still had a rich circulation of gold coinages. Figure 15 shows the distribution of some late gold series that were in full circulation in the mid-first century BC. There is still debate among archaeologists and numisma-tists about the precise chronology of the youngest gold emissions (Haselgrove 2019; Roymans 2019b). For some coin series an extended chronology with a start in the decades preceding the conquest is plausible. For other series, however, a short chronology largely corresponding with the conquest period is more convincing. The overall impression is that gold circulation reached a peak in the mid-first century BC and almost came to an end in that same period. By quantifying the number of coin dies used for each

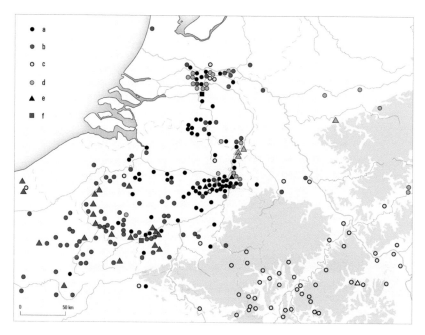

Figure 15 Distribution of some Late Iron Age gold coins that were in full circulation in the conquest period. a. staters type Scheers 31 ('Eburones'); b. staters type Scheers 29 ('Nervii'); c. staters type Scheers 30-IV/V ('Treveri'); d. electrum/ silver rainbow staters type Lith; e. hoard find; f. sanctuary (image: N. Roymans, based on Roymans and Scheers 2012; Hornung 2016, with additions)

coin type, we get an idea of the size of the emissions, thereby assuming a production rate of at least 1,000 coins per obverse die (Roymans and Scheers 2012). The volumes of the different emissions show considerable variation, but it is clear that several hundred thousand gold coins must have been circulating in the northern half of Belgic Gaul at the time of the conquest.

The mid-first century BC corresponds with a significant peak in hoard deposition (Roymans 2019b; Roymans and Scheers 2012) (Figure 16). It seems reasonable to associate this 'hoard horizon' with the extreme circumstances of war that Caesar describes for this northern region. A second observation is that – in contrast to the situation observable in Britain – there is hardly any evidence for a continuation of the production and circulation of gold coins in the post-conquest period (Roymans 1990). After Caesar's departure, gold circulation almost disappeared in this frontier zone. The most plausible interpretation is that the 'disappearance' of the indigenous gold was a direct consequence of a systematic extraction of precious metals by

Figure 16 The gold hoard of Thuin-1, containing 73 staters ascribed to the
Nervii (photo: Fondation Roi Baudouin, Brussels)

Caesar via plundering, ransom payments, and forced tribute payments. This
underlines the importance of the economic dimension of Caesar's campaigns
in Gaul.

2.7 The Decades after the Conquest

The written sources scarcely inform us about the situation in *Gallia Comata* in
the decades after Caesar's departure. Caesar had imposed on Gaul
a substantial tribute of 40 million *sestertii* per year (Suetonius *Jul.* 25) and
continued to exploit the military potential of Gallic societies. It is generally
assumed that Rome controlled the newly conquered regions through a system
of small garrisons stationed in some Gallic *oppida* and consisting of legionaries and/or Gallic auxiliaries (Reddé 2022). Archaeological indicators of
Roman military presence (*militaria*, Republican *denarii*, Gallic silver *qui-
narii*) have been encountered in the *oppida* of Chaussée-Tirancourt in northwest France and at the Titelberg in Luxemburg, where bronze coinage
inscribed with the name of Aulus Hirtius was minted around 45 BC. We also
hear about local unrest in Gaul. The *Treveri* revolted in 30–29 BC, an uprising
that probably corresponded with the construction of a large Roman army camp
on the Petrisberg at Trier (Löhr 2018) and the burning down of the Roman
trading post on the Titelberg (Metzler et al. 2018).

But it is important to consider that in many *civitates* the anti-Roman factions
had been eliminated or at least largely decimated in the course of the Gallic

Wars. This created opportunities for aristocrats who were willing to support Caesar, thereby hoping for rewards in the form of land, wealth, and local political power. After the conquest, loyal Gallic aristocrats and their war bands followed Caesar in the Civil Wars. This auxiliary service of Gallic horsemen is also archaeologically traceable (Pernet 2019), for example in the Treveran elite cemetery of Goeblingen-Nospelt. The burials of the first generation of auxiliaries often contain a mixture of weapons from both Gallic and Roman traditions.

We should not underestimate the social effects of large-scale Gallic auxiliary service in the 40s and 30s BC. It deprived Gaul of a generation of warriors that could potentially have fuelled local revolts, and the subsequent reduced military potential would have strengthened the position of pro-Roman aristocrats in their homelands. Rewarded with money, land, and Roman citizenship, they were instrumental in the process of integration into the Roman world and the introduction of a new provincial order under Augustus. In many regions, this pro-Roman Gallic elite rapidly transformed into a civil elite in the Augustan period. Only among Germanic groups in the far north can we observe a continuation of the old system of intensive military exploitation by Rome, as exemplified with the *Batavi* (Roymans 2004).

3 The Last Frontier in Iberia: The Cantabrian and Asturian Wars

3.1 The Roman Conquest of Iberia: A Long Process

The Roman conquest of the Iberian Peninsula was a long process that lasted for about 200 years (Cadiou and Navarro-Caballero 2014). It started in 218 BC, when Roman troops arrived at the Greek colony of *Emporion* in northeast Iberia with the goal of fighting against the Carthaginians in the context of the Second Punic War, and concluded in 19 BC with the victory over the last independent populations of northern Iberia at the end of the Cantabrian and Asturian Wars. Between these two events, numerous military campaigns and rebellions took place across *Hispania* (Figure 17). While the Mediterranean regions were conquered relatively rapidly (although not without some violent encounters and rebellions, as exemplified by the Battle of *Emporion* in 195 BC), the populations of inner Iberia were the ones that offered the longest and fiercest resistance against the Roman power. Particularly significant were the Celtiberian and Lusitanian Wars in the second century BC, which included the famous episodes of the fall of the Celtiberian city of *Numantia* in 133 BC and the assassination of the Lusitanian leader Viriathus in 139 BC. Both events became important elements in the construction of Spanish nationalism from the nineteenth century to the Franco dictatorship (Ruiz Zapatero 2016), as examples of heroic resistance against an external invader – a phenomenon not dissimilar to

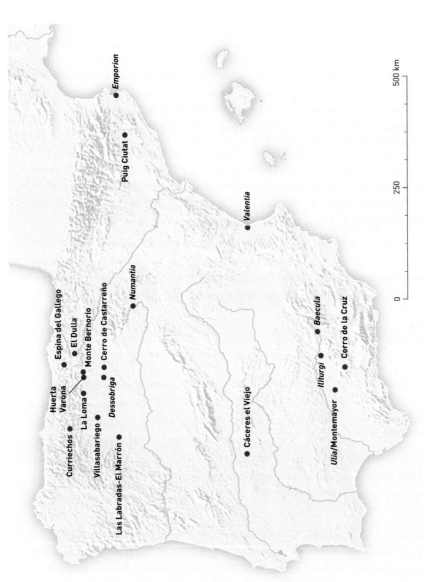

Figure 17 Location of the main sites mentioned in Section 3 (authors)

the erection of the statues of Vercingetorix, Arminius, and Boudica mentioned in Sections 2, 4, and 5, respectively.

In addition to the plethora of written sources that provide extremely valuable – although also biased – accounts of the various wars, since the nineteenth century archaeology has also been contributing to our knowledge of the Roman conquest of Iberia. Particularly famous are the extensive archaeological investigations carried out on the siege of *Numantia*, from the work of Schulten in the early twentieth century to the present (Jiménez et al. 2020). In line with the growth of conflict archaeology, the last few decades have experienced a veritable 'explosion' in the quantity and quality of archaeological discoveries related to the Roman wars in Iberia (Morillo et al. 2020; Quesada 2019). The investigations related to the Second Punic War have been especially fruitful, including several key scenarios mentioned in written sources, most notably in Catalonia (Noguera et al. 2013) and in the province of Jaén. In the latter, the identification and study of the Battle of *Baecula* (208 BC) represent a milestone for battlefield archaeology in Iberia (Bellón et al. 2015). Research on the Second Punic War has not been limited to the clash between the two superpowers of the Western Mediterranean, but has also explored the repercussions on indigenous communities, including punitive actions of the Romans, for example in the case of the siege and destruction of the *oppidum* of *Iliturgi* in 206 BC (Bellón et al. 2021). In later decades, veritable massacres committed by the Roman army have been documented at indigenous sites such as Cerro de la Cruz, where several bodies show signs of torture and amputations, probably as part of a retaliation campaign dated to around the mid-second century BC (Quesada 2021) (Figure 18).

Archaeology has not only revealed scenarios of direct conquest, but has also provided interesting insights into the Roman Civil Wars that affected large areas of Iberia at various points of the first century BC. Particularly profound was the impact of the Sertorian Wars (82–72 BC), during which many indigenous groups allied with the rebel Quintus Sertorius, which led to retaliations by the Roman state after his defeat. Archaeologically, information on the Sertorian Wars has come mainly from military camps (e.g. Cáceres el Viejo) as well as from sieges and the destruction of sites (e.g. *Valentia*) (Morillo and Sala 2019; Noguera et al. 2022). Moreover, there is increasing archaeological evidence related to the confrontation between Julius Caesar and Pompey the Great and his sons around the mid-first century BC. Examples of the latter include the destruction of the site of Puig Ciutat in Catalonia, probably as part of the military operations that preceded the Battle of *Ilerda* in 49 BC (Pujol et al. 2019), and the identification of the battlefields at *Ulia*/Montemayor related to combat in 48 BC and 45 BC (Quesada and Moralejo-Ordax 2020).

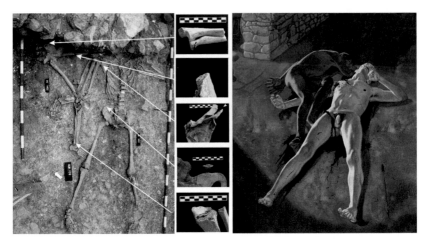

Figure 18 Cerro de la Cruz. Left: two skeletons with perimortem injuries. Right: artist's recreation of the bodies of the two dead adult males, who were violently killed and left on one of the main streets of the settlement together with at least five more women and men in close proximity (after Quesada 2021; drawing: S. Delgado, Desperta Ferro Ediciones)

3.2 The Cantabrian and Asturian Wars: Sources and Motivations

The last episode of the Roman conquest of Iberia were the Cantabrian and Asturian Wars (*Bellum Cantabricum et Asturicum*) that took place between 29 and 19 BC, i.e. just about one generation after Caesar's Gallic Wars. The military operations were focused on the territory of the current northern Spanish regions of Cantabria and Asturias, as well as the northern part of Castilla y León (provinces of Burgos, Palencia, and León), probably with some occasional activity in Galicia (Figure 19). The *Cantabri* and the *Astures* occupied not only the area of the Cantabrian Mountains, but also some territories to their immediate south, which is where their most important *oppida* (such as Monte Bernorio, La Loma, and *Lancia*) were located.

The conquest campaigns were carried out immediately after the end of the Roman Civil Wars, representing the only conflict that Augustus fought in person against foreign enemies after the beginning of the Principate. Other important historical figures of the period, such as Agrippa, also participated directly in these military actions. Because of this, the Cantabrian and Asturian Wars probably featured prominently in ancient written sources. Unfortunately, Livy's description of the *Bellum Cantabricum et Asturicum* has been lost, which leaves references by Florus, Orosius, and Cassius Dio as the main

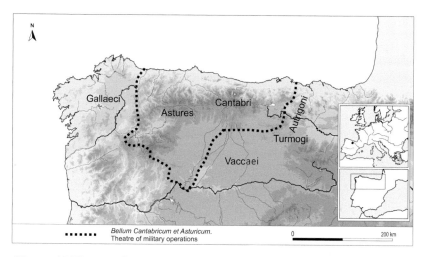

Figure 19 Theatre of military operations during the *Bellum Cantabricum et Asturicum* (map drawn by IMBEAC & A. Martínez-Velasco, modified by authors).

available classical sources, supplemented by mentions in the works of a few other authors such as Strabo (cf. González-Echegaray 1999).

The Cantabrian and Asturian Wars played an important role in the consolidation of the Principate (Griffiths 2013). The fight against an external enemy was an effective way to unite forces after the long period of the first century BC Civil Wars that had substantially affected the Roman state. Augustus had already emerged as the victor against other Roman leaders such as Marcus Antonius. With the conquest of the last free communities of northern Iberia, he could also present himself as a conqueror of 'barbarians'. The official justification for the wars was that the *Cantabri* and *Astures* had launched raids against neighbouring tribes that were already under Roman control. Without denying the possible existence of some raids, it is necessary to go beyond this official narrative imbued with broader *topoi* and elements of propaganda, and acknowledge that the main motivations for the Roman intervention would have been political (increasing Augustus' personal prestige, helping to consolidate the new regime) and economic (particularly gaining access to the rich metal resources of the northern regions, such as gold) (Amela 2013–14; Griffiths 2013). Moreover, it has been proposed that the control of the Cantabrian Sea and its harbours would have been beneficial for securing the supply lines along the Atlantic coast for the future Augustan campaigns in *Germania* (Ramos and Jiménez 2015).

Similar to the situation documented in the northernmost regions of Gaul (see Sections 2.4–2.6), the Cantabrian and Asturian Wars witnessed the most brutal side of Roman imperialism. According to Cassius Dio (53.29.2), the land of the *Cantabri* was devastated. In addition to cases of large-scale destruction and enslavement, the conquest included some macabre episodes such as cutting off the hands of defeated Cantabrian fighters. Many *Cantabri* went so far as to choose to commit suicide rather than surrender to the Roman troops (Cassius Dio 54.5.1–3). What might have initially been conceived of as a triumphant march ultimately became a costly military effort for Rome. Seven or eight Roman legions plus auxiliary troops and ten years of war were required in order to subjugate the *Cantabri* and *Astures*, as well as the last free communities of the *Vaccaei* and the *Gallaeci*. The fact that both Augustus and Agrippa declined to celebrate the triumphs that were offered to them might be indicative, among other aspects, of the challenges encountered by the Roman army in northern Iberia.

While ancient authors clearly highlight the fierceness of the resistance by the indigenous populations and the brutality of the Roman military actions, for a long time many scholars underestimated the real impact of these wars on local communities. This was largely due to the scarcity of material remains that could be associated with the campaigns, which remained largely invisible from an archaeological point of view. However, this situation has fundamentally changed in the last few decades. Since the 1990s, the work of different research teams has revolutionised our knowledge of the materiality of these veritable 'mountain wars' (cf. overviews in Camino et al. 2015; Peralta et al. 2019). The discoveries include not only several dozen Roman military camps dating from the period of the Cantabrian and Asturian Wars and their aftermath (many of them identified through aerial photography and LiDAR, cf. Martín-Hernández et al. 2020; Menéndez-Blanco et al. 2020) (Figure 20), but also evidence for the violent destruction of important indigenous strongholds such as Monte Bernorio (Fernández-Götz et al. 2018) and La Loma (Peralta et al. 2022). In what follows, we will summarise some of the main evidence related to these military campaigns in the far north of Iberia, which have yielded archaeological remains that are among the most impressive of all the Roman wars of conquest in Western Europe. This is also reinforced by the intricate topography of the Cantabrian Mountains, with several key war scenarios located at spectacular locations, often at an altitude of over 1,000 m.

3.3 The Beginning of the War: From the 29 BC Campaign to the Arrival of Augustus

The history of military encounters between Rome and the *Cantabri* goes back well beyond the final wars of conquest (Peralta 2003). For example, there is evidence that the *Cantabri* helped the *Vaccaei* in 151 BC and aided the besieged

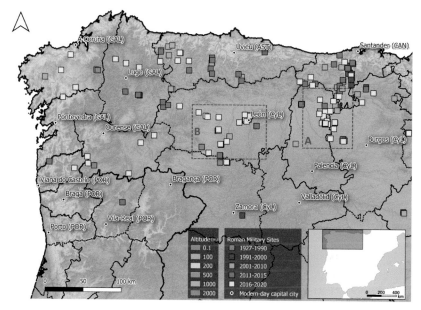

Figure 20 Roman military sites archaeologically attested in northwestern Iberia according to their discovery/publication date (after Menéndez-Blanco et al. 2020)

Celtiberian city of *Numantia* in 137 BC. In the first century BC, some Cantabrian groups were at least sporadically involved in the Roman Civil Wars that took place in Iberia, and they also seemed to have helped the *Aquitani* in their war against Rome in 56 BC.

In any case, the final military operations that led to the submission of the last independent populations of northern Iberia started in 29 BC, with a campaign led by Statilius Taurus against the *Vaccaei*, the *Cantabri*, and the *Astures* (Cassius Dio 51.20.4–5; see also Amela 2013–14; Perea Yébenes 2017). Our knowledge of this initial confrontation is very limited. Archaeologically, some evidence from the *oppidum* of *Dessobriga* has been linked with this campaign. Although many communities of the *Vaccaei* had already been conquered several decades earlier, other groups still remained outside Roman control. This could have been the case at *Dessobriga*, where finds including a Gallic coin and Roman *militaria* uncovered in one of the defensive ditches of the *oppidum* and dating to the years of the Late Republic and/or Early Principate suggest an assault on the site by Roman troops, perhaps as part of the initial offensive by Statilius Taurus (Torrione 2018; Torrione and Cahanier 2014) (Figure 21).

The main operations of the Cantabrian and Asturian Wars began in 26 BC, when Augustus himself went to *Hispania* to oversee the military campaigns.

Figure 21 Roman *militaria* and Gallic coin found at *Dessobriga*
(after Torrione 2018)

The fact that in the *Res Gestae Divi Augusti* (29) he mentions the recovery of
military standards that had been lost by other generals suggests that there were
some Roman military setbacks in the years preceding his arrival. The Emperor
established his headquarters in *Segisama* (possibly located in or around the area
of present-day Sasamón), from which the main offensive against the *Cantabri*
was launched. The years 26–25 BC were crucial for the development of the war
(Morillo 2014), with major Roman victories at the battles of *Bergida* against the
Cantabri and *Lancia* in the territory of the *Astures*.

Recent archaeological research in the immediate vicinity of Sasamón has
revealed spectacular evidence for a Roman siege system around the indigenous
oppidum of Cerro de Castarreño, a major Late Iron Age site of over 20 ha
(Costa-García and García-Sánchez in press; García-Sánchez et al. 2022)
(Figure 22). While the precise dating of this event remains challenging, it is
very likely that the siege was associated with military activity in the 30s BC or
early 20s BC, perhaps even in 29 BC as part of the aforementioned campaign of
Statilius Taurus. Be that as it may, this new evidence – to which some Roman
military finds discovered in the *oppidum* itself should be added – clearly defies
previous conceptions of a relatively peaceful incorporation of the *Turmogi* into
the Roman Empire. In imperial times, the main settlement activity moved to the
newly founded Roman town of *Segisamo*, located nearby on the plain. This
move from a pre-Roman *oppidum* on a hill to a new Roman foundation on the
plain resembles the situation in many other regions after the Roman conquest.

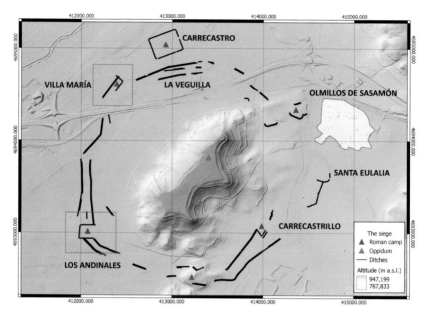

Figure 22 The siege of Cerro de Castarreño. Late Iron Age *oppidum* (blue triangle), Roman camps (red triangles), siege structures (black lines), and the extent of the modern-day town of Olmillos de Sasamón (white area) (after Costa-García and García-Sánchez in press)

3.4 The Destruction of the *Oppida* of Monte Bernorio and La Loma

From his base in *Segisama*, Emperor Augustus divided his troops into three columns, which attacked the territory of the *Cantabri* heading north on different fronts. Probably conscious of the superiority of the Roman army in an open battle, the indigenous communities opted for taking refuge in their hillforts and *oppida*, from where they exerted pressure using tactics of guerrilla warfare. However, and despite the challenges posed by the warlike *Cantabri*, the highly experienced and numerically superior Roman army was ultimately able to take control of various key indigenous fortifications. While the enormous *oppidum* of La Ulaña – with its upper platform of nearly 300 ha that would have been difficult to defend against a large army – might have been abandoned intentionally (although not necessarily voluntarily; cf. Setién and Cisneros 2023), other settlements show clear signs of a Roman attack. Indeed, the archaeological research from the last few decades has uncovered substantial evidence for the violent destruction of several Cantabrian strongholds, most notably Monte Bernorio and La Loma, which controlled important access routes to the mountain passes.

The *oppidum* of Monte Bernorio has a long settlement history, which can be traced back to the Bronze Age. Located on a communication crossroads at the centre of the foothills of the Cantabrian Mountains, by the first century BC it was one of the main centres of the *Cantabri* (Torres-Martínez et al. 2016). The settlement occupied the relatively flat summit and lower terraces of a limestone mountain over 1,100 m high (Figure 23). At the end of the Iron Age, the upper part of the mountain was fortified by a ditch and rampart that enclosed an area of 28 ha. In addition, a number of large concentric earthworks on the slopes and the foot of the mountain formed a multivallate system that expanded the area of the *oppidum* to at least 90 ha. Fieldwork at Monte Bernorio has uncovered houses, burials, and large quantities of materials such as pottery, animal bones, and metalwork, testifying to the intensity of occupation and the wide-ranging contacts of the local inhabitants.

However, the long settlement trajectory of Monte Bernorio was brutally aborted when the site was attacked by the Roman army during the course of the Cantabrian Wars (Fernández-Götz et al. 2018). Just a few kilometres in front of the *oppidum*, a large Roman camp known as El Castillejo has been identified (Peralta 2004). With an area of over 40 ha, it is one of the largest temporary camps known in Western Europe. Finds from El Castillejo include, among others, *caligae* nails, arrowheads, a *pilum*, bronze artefacts related to military dress, tent pole fragments, as well as coins that date the site to the Early Principate of Augustus. Given its size, the camp could have accommodated at least two legions with accompanying auxiliaries. From this camp the Romans would have launched the attack on Monte Bernorio.

Figure 23 The Bernorio Mountain, in the background the Cantabrian Mountains (© IMBEAC; photo: D. Vacas)

On the *oppidum* itself, excavations have demonstrated that the site was assaulted and destroyed by Roman forces (Brown et al. 2017; Fernández-Götz et al. 2018). A massive fire identifiable through abundant ash, charcoal, and burnt or carbonised artefacts marks the end of the indigenous occupation. The discovery of numerous projectiles confirms the use of artillery by the attacking Roman army. Some of the arrowheads have even been found stuck to the outer face of the wall, or at its base. Moreover, elements of Roman typology including *caligae* nails and two pieces of legionary soldiers' finger rings have been recovered. Overall, the evidence clearly suggests that the *oppidum* fell after a battle on the southern side of Monte Bernorio (Figure 24). It is tempting to identify this event with the battle of *Bergida* mentioned in written sources. According to Florus (2.33.49), the main battle against the *Cantabri* was fought under the walls of *Bergida*, a description that would fit well with a confrontation in the area of the multivallate fortification system at the foot of the Bernorio mountain. Following the conquest, the Roman army established a *castellum* on the northwestern part of the mountain, which lasted for some decades in order to control the territory in the post-war period. But apart from this military installation, Monte Bernorio was never resettled. It only became relevant again in the context of the Spanish Civil War, when due to its strategic position it witnessed intensive military activity in 1936–1937. Thus, at Monte Bernorio we have two important battlefields at the same location, separated by nearly two millennia.

Another key site for our understanding of the Roman conquest of the *Cantabri* is the *oppidum* of La Loma, which comprises a fortified area of nearly 17 ha. The archaeological investigations of the last two decades have identified an impressive Roman siege system, which surrounded the *oppidum* and was composed of a main camp of ca. 9 ha and two smaller *castella* (Peralta 2015; Peralta et al. 2022). The Roman attack on the indigenous settlement is attested by numerous finds of *militaria* identified at the *oppidum* and the Roman camps, most strikingly the discovery of more than 2,000 Roman arrowheads showcasing a diverse range of typologies. The assemblage of Roman and indigenous military finds recovered at La Loma is among the most important found in the whole of Europe. After the destruction of the *oppidum*, and similar to the case of Monte Bernorio, the Romans established a *castellum*.

With the conquest of Monte Bernorio and Loma, the Roman army would have controlled the main access routes into the Cantabrian Mountains. Within the inner mountain range, further evidence of Roman camps and conquered indigenous settlements has been identified archaeologically (Peralta et al. 2019), for example the hillfort of Espina del Gallego and the nearby Roman camp of Cildá (Peralta 2001). In addition to the south–north advance through the mountains, some Roman troops also arrived by sea disembarking at the so-called *Portus*

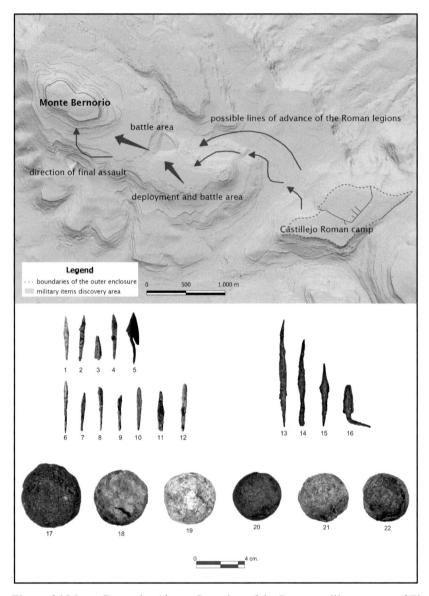

Figure 24 Monte Bernorio. Above: Location of the Roman military camp of El Castillejo and possible direction of the attack on the *oppidum* (© IMBEAC; design: J.F. Torres-Martínez and A. Solana-Muñoz, modified by authors). Below: Selection of Roman projectiles found at Monte Bernorio (© IMBEAC; design: J.F. Torres-Martínez and M. Galeano)

Victoriae (probably Santander). Despite their fierce resistance, the *Cantabri* came under intense pressure from multiple fronts and were finally defeated.

3.5 War in the West: The Campaigns against the Astures

In addition to the offensives against the *Cantabri*, further to the west the Roman army under the command of Publius Carisius launched an attack against the *Astures*. The most famous event of the initial confrontations was the defeat of the *Astures* at *Lancia* (probably in 25 BC), which according to Cassius Dio (53.25.8) represented their most important *oppidum*. Following Florus (2.33.54–59) and other writers, the *Astures* assembled a large army that tried to attack three Roman winter camps (*castra hiberna*). However, the Romans, after having been warned of these plans by the *Brigaecini*, marched against the *Astures* and defeated them. After the battle, the remaining contingents of the *Astures* took refuge in *Lancia*, but Publius Carisius followed them and ultimately took the stronghold. Unlike what happened to Monte Bernorio and La Loma in the area of the *Cantabri*, Publius Carisius gave orders to respect the settlement rather than to destroy it. Archaeologically, *Lancia* is identified by most scholars with the ca. 30 ha *oppidum* located in Villasabariego. Late Iron Age remains have indeed been found there, although most of the known evidence comes from the town that existed in Roman times.

The account of the conquest of *Lancia* and the battle that preceded it demonstrates not only that the *Astures* were able to bring together an army of considerable size, but also that they were far from constituting a homogenous group, as testified by the betrayal of the *Brigaecini*, who were part of the *Astures Cismontani*. This reminds us of the complexity of indigenous social structures and how not only different tribes, but also subgroups within them, could respond in divergent ways to their encounters with the Roman power – a phenomenon also observable in the other case studies discussed in this volume. In northern Gaul, for example, only some *pagi* of the *Morini* sent ambassadors to meet Caesar and reach an agreement with him in 55 BC, whereas others refused to do so (*BG* 4.22).

Another very important archaeological site situated in the southern territory of the *Astures* is the *oppidum* of Las Labradas-El Marrón, which some authors have recently proposed as an alternative location for *Lancia*. In the first century BC, Las Labradas-El Marrón occupied an area of more than 40 ha. Two impressive hoards, known as the 'treasures of Arrabalde' and composed of a large number of gold and silver objects, were found at the site in the 1980s (Delibes et al. 1996). The hoards, which include some of the most outstanding examples of pre-Roman jewellery in central and northern Spain (Figure 25), were probably buried in the context of the Roman conquest of the region. Furthermore, a Roman camp and a possible *castellum* have recently been identified in the proximity of Las Labradas-El Marrón, suggesting a siege of the *oppidum* by the Roman army. Elements of Roman *militaria* have also been discovered within the indigenous site (Hierro et al. 2019).

Figure 25 Treasure I of Arrabalde (© Museo de Zamora)

Moving further north, in the territory of the current Autonomous Community of Asturias, the advance of the Roman troops through the mountains has been well documented along south–north lines that can be traced thanks to the discovery of various Roman camps, for example at the so-called Vía Carisa. This Roman road, built by order of Publius Carisius, runs through high altitudes ranging at some points between 1,500 and 1,800 m. Particularly significant is the Roman camp of Curriechos, where investigations have uncovered military objects such as *pila catapultaria*, spearheads, and tent pegs, as well as coins including an *as* of Publius Carisius (Camino 2015; Camino and Martín-Hernández 2014). This camp is located at an altitude of over 1,700 m, making it one of the highest ever found in Europe. Like several other Roman camps in northern Spain, it had more than one occupation phase, which demonstrates its use beyond the initial military conquest campaign. In any case, the discoveries show that the Roman army primarily advanced through this part of Asturias along mountain ridges, rather than through the bottom of the valleys.

3.6 Final Uprisings and Post-conquest Developments

While the campaigns of the years 26–25 BC culminated in significant Roman victories against the *Cantabri* and the *Astures*, the conflict was far from over. Several indigenous uprisings took place in the following years, as attested by both written sources and archaeological evidence. For example, a major revolt of the *Astures* occurred in 22 BC, an event with which the refortification of the Roman camp of Curriechos has been linked (Camino 2015). In the same year, the *Cantabri* also revolted.

Another major uprising is documented in 19 BC, when some enslaved Cantabrians that had managed to escape started a new rebellion. The uprising was so important that Agrippa had to be sent to the region to control the situation, which he only achieved after heavy fighting, some setbacks, and significant losses on both sides. According to written sources, this campaign by Agrippa witnessed some of the 'darkest sides' of Roman imperialism, as well as frequent episodes of suicide by *Cantabri* who chose death over surrender. According to Cassius Dio (54.11.5–6), Agrippa 'at length destroyed nearly all of the enemy who were of military age, deprived the rest of their arms, and forced them to come down from their fortresses and live in the plains'. Probably related to this campaign is the episode documented at El Dulla, a plateau surrounded by cliffs in which some rebels took refuge. They were besieged by Roman camps including the one at La Muela and finally attacked, as attested by projectiles (Bohigas et al. 2015). There is mention of a final indigenous rebellion in 16 BC, although it seems to have been supressed rather quickly.

The decades after the completion of the conquest have been designated as a period of 'armed peace' (Morillo 2017). Three legions (*IV Macedonica, VI Victrix,* and *X Gemina*) were stationed in the territory to control the situation and several large base camps developed (most notably Herrera de Pisuerga, León, and Astorga). The Romans also began to exploit the extremely rich mineral resources of the region, which would have represented one of the main incentives for the war and were instrumental in supporting Augustus' coinage reform. Some of the post-conquest military presence in the northwest seems to have supported gold mining activities, as well as helped to establish and maintain the infrastructure network (Beltrán et al. 2019). Regarding the situation of the indigenous communities, most of them would have been dramatically affected by the war. However, a few groups that had allied during the campaigns with the Romans were rewarded after the conflict, as shown in the 'Bierzo Edict' from 15 BC (Alföldy 2000).

Finally, archaeology is also providing new information on the development of settlement activity in the post-conquest period. A recently investigated example is the site of Huerta Varona. This settlement is located on the plain just a few kilometres away from Monte Bernorio, and seems to have become the main population centre in the area after the violent destruction of the *oppidum* (Torres-Martínez et al. 2019). The abundant finds date Huerta Varona to between the late first century BC (probably founded during the Cantabrian

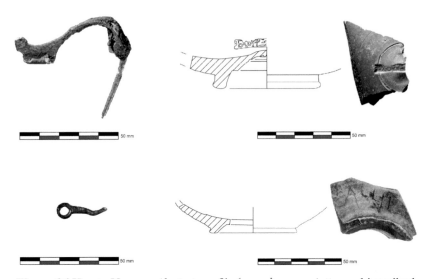

Figure 26 Huerta Varona: *Alesia*-type fibula, make-up palette, and inscribed fragments of *terra sigillata* (© IMBEAC)

Wars or immediately afterwards) and Late Antiquity. Some metal objects, such as an *Alesia*-type fibula, *caligae* nails, and weaponry fragments, suggest a Roman military origin for the settlement, which seems to have developed into a *vicus* (Figure 26).

4 The Germanic Wars of Augustus: A Failed Imperial Project

4.1 History of the Romano-Germanic Confrontations

The Germanic Wars of Emperor Augustus, which had their absolute climax in the defeat of Varus in the Teutoburg Forest in AD 9, have figured among the most prominent themes of German national history for about five centuries now. The victory gained by a coalition of Germanic tribes under the leadership of the Cheruscan chief Arminius has been repeatedly used as a symbol and source of inspiration for political ambitions and identity construction (Burmeister 2021; Zelle 2015). In the sixteenth century, German humanists presented Augustus' Germanic Wars as an analogy for the fight for freedom against the Habsburg Empire, while in the context of nineteenth century German nationalism the hero Arminius figured as a symbol of German political unification and military strength (Figure 27).

However, what do we actually know about the Romano-Germanic confrontations on the basis of historical and archaeological data? In this section, we provide an overview of the current state of research, addressing in particular the following

Figure 27 Hermann's Monument (*Hermannsdenkmal*) near Detmold, constructed between 1838 and 1875 to commemorate the victory of Arminius in AD 9 (photo: M. Fernández-Götz)

questions: how did the conflict develop?; what is the material record of the wars?; and why did the Roman expansion policy ultimately fail?

Augustus' Germanic Wars need to be understood within the wider framework of Rome's imperialist expansion, which in this area started as a defensive strategy to counter incursions of Germanic groups in Gaul but over time developed into an imperial policy to conquer the area between the rivers Rhine and Elbe (Figure 28). The Roman military confrontation with Germanic groups has an even deeper history that starts with the Cimbrian Wars (113–101 BC). A coalition of *Cimbri* and *Teutones* originating in Jutland and Northern Germany adopted a migratory way of life and crossed much of Central and Western Europe. They soon formed a direct threat to Rome's provinces and allies. Initially Rome suffered some crushing defeats, especially in 105 BC at *Arausio*/Orange in Transalpine Gaul, but after fundamental reorganisations of the Roman army by Gaius Marius, the *Cimbri* and *Teutones* were finally beaten in 102 and 101 BC.

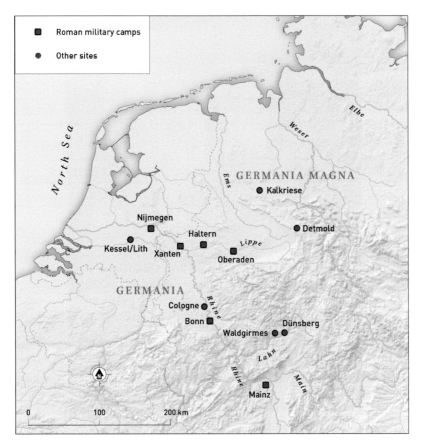

Figure 28 Location of the main sites mentioned in Section 4 (authors)

Caesar's conquest of Gaul was the next phase in Rome's confrontation with Germanic groups that had crossed the Rhine and entered Gaul. In 58 BC he defeated the Germanic war leader Ariovistus, and in 55 BC he destroyed the *Tencteri* and *Usipetes*, which had asked for permission to settle in Gaul but were refused (see Section 2.4). In 55 and 53 BC, Caesar himself crossed the Rhine in order to punish Germanic groups on the east bank for their involvement in anti-Roman coalitions in northern Gaul.

In the decades after Caesar's departure from Gaul, the continued pressure of Germanic groups on the Rhine sometimes triggered Roman generals to cross the river for short 'defensive' expeditions into *Germania*. In 16 BC, the defeat of an army led by Marcus Lollius became a turning point in the imperial policy and led to large-scale offensives against Germanic groups from 12 BC onwards, probably with the aim of conquering the entire area between the Rhine and Elbe to transform it into a province named *Germania*. This ambition required several decades of huge investments of manpower and finances by Rome. A series of army camps along the rivers Rhine and Lippe formed the backbone of the Roman military infrastructure during the Germanic Wars. Well known are the offensives led by Drusus (12–9 BC) and Tiberius (AD 4–5) (cf. Rudnick 2017; Wolters 2017). The turning point was the defeat of Varus in AD 9 (Figure 29). This event was followed by a series of revenge campaigns by Tiberius and Germanicus between AD 10 and 16, until Emperor Tiberius ordered a general withdrawal of Roman troops from the area. With the creation of the Rhine *limes*, this river again became the formal border of the Empire.

4.2 Putting into Perspective Some Roman Stereotypes of the Germanic 'Other'

Our image of Germans and the Romano-Germanic Wars is heavily based on Roman written sources, and therefore primarily reflects a Roman perspective. This becomes clear when we consider the origin of the ethnic term *Germani* and the geographic term *Germania* (Lund 1998). As is often the case in imperial

Figure 29 Grave monument from Xanten of Marcus Caelius, *centurio* who fell in the *bello Variano*, either at the Varus Battle of AD 9 or an undocumented battle from the previous two years of Varus' governorship
(image: J. Vogel, LVR-LandesMuseum Bonn)

contexts, ethnic macro-labels of peripheral groups are largely filled-in by the imperial power itself. Initially, the term *Germani* formed an indigenous ascriptive label for a small group of culturally related tribes inhabiting both banks of the Lower Rhine. Then Caesar introduced a new macro-definition of *Germani* that included all peoples living east of the Rhine and defined this river as the natural boundary between a Gallic and a Germanic block. For the latter he introduced the geographical term *Germania*.

Archaeology, however, has demonstrated that the Germanic groups did not form a homogenous cultural entity, but exhibited substantial regional differences (Burmeister 2020). A basic distinction can be made between peoples living along the Rhine south and north of the Lippe. In the pre-Roman period, many communities south of the Lippe were strongly influenced by the 'Celtic' La Tène culture and had adopted coinage, wheel-turned pottery, mass-production of metal and glass ornaments, and in some cases *oppida* functioning as tribal centres. On the other hand, the peoples north of the Lippe and further east of the Rhine had less developed social hierarchies and a much lower level of connectivity with the La Tène culture and the Roman world. According to written sources, the 'Rhine-Germanic' groups were under continuous military pressure from the more eastern groups.

It is important to relate the written accounts of the Germanic Wars to a set of highly stereotypical images of the Germanic 'Other' in the Roman sources (Lund 1998; Von See 1981). *Germani* are depicted as the ultimate 'barbarians', not receptive of civilisation and driven by a lust for war and plunder. The image of *Germani* as warlike, migratory peoples was repeatedly actualised by reports of migrations and raiding parties of Germanic groups into Gallic territories. However, the deeper causes for this drive to migrate were not considered. In the Roman discourse it was simply explained as an intrinsic trait of Germanic ethnicity and way of life. The deeper causes, however, can be sought in the socio-economic sphere. In Büntgen's reconstruction of long-term fluctuations in temperature and precipitation (Figure 30), the period of the Germanic Wars is characterised by a colder and drier climate (Büntgen et al. 2011). The sandy landscapes of the Northwest European Plain were not only impacted by climate change, but also faced with the structural problem of soil degradation. Such environmental challenges contributed to a situation of societal stress, which is expressed above all in the large-scale abandonment of so-called Celtic field complexes on the marginal sandy soils (Roymans 2023).

4.3 Exploring the Materiality of the Germanic Wars

Our knowledge of the Germanic Wars is primarily based on written documentation. Archaeology, however, has contributed in several ways to the study of this conflict.

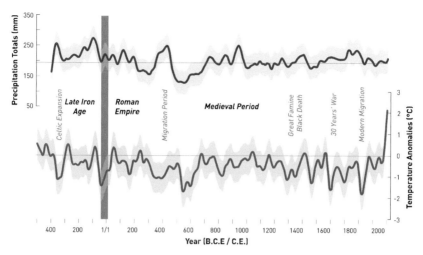

Figure 30 Reconstructed precipitation totals (top) and temperature anomalies (bottom) in Central and Northwest Europe over the past 2,500 years. The period of the Germanic Wars of Augustus is marked by a vertical red bar (redrawn after Büntgen et al. 2011)

Most successful have been attempts to identify Roman camps and other elements of Roman military infrastructure, helped by the easily recognisable Roman material culture and spatial layout of the camps. Much energy has been invested in the development of a detailed typo-chronological framework of small finds, in particular fine pottery and Roman coins. Such analyses often allow an ascription of military sites to a specific sub-period of the Germanic Wars, which (at a higher level) may contribute to the geographical reconstruction of specific military campaigns and the associated supply lines of the Roman army (Burmeister 2015; Rudnick 2017).

The earliest examples of Roman camps east of the Rhine have been documented at Limburg along the Lahn River (Hesse). The two camps can be connected to Caesar's Rhine crossings of 55 and/or 53 BC (Hornung 2021). Further north, the analysis of the coin finds from the Augustan *castra* at Nijmegen-Hunerberg (Kemmers 2008) points to a construction of the fortress around 20 BC, suggesting a link with the campaign of Agrippa across the Rhine in 20/19 BC. In the context of this operation, Agrippa relocated the *Ubii* and possibly also the *Batavi* from the east to the west bank of the Rhine. Between 12 and 9 BC the military operations carried out by Drusus marked the start of the large-scale *Germania* offensives of Augustus, aimed at the conquest of territories up to the Elbe. A series of military bases from the middle-Augustan period (including Nijmegen-Kops Plateau, Xanten-*Vetera* and Mainz along the Rhine, and Haltern and Oberaden along the Lippe) can be linked to Drusus and have been used in attempts to reconstruct his campaigns (Rudnick 2017) (Figure 31).

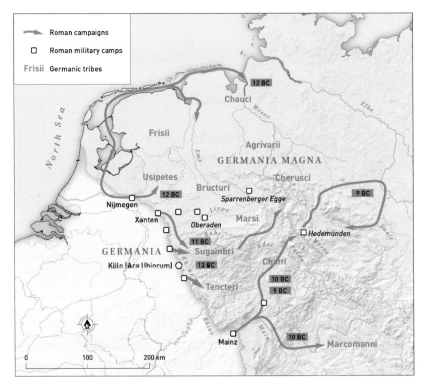

Figure 31 Tribal map of *Germania* at the time of Augustus and reconstruction of the offensives by Drusus (12–9 BC) (redrawn after Burmeister 2015, with some modifications)

A challenge for archaeology is the identification of historically documented battlefields. An intriguing project is currently being carried out at Orange in southern France, where archaeologists may have identified the battlefield of *Arausio* where the *Cimbri* and *Teutones* defeated a large Roman army in 105 BC (Deyber and Luginbühl 2018). Another interesting site is Kessel-Lith in the Dutch river delta, where large numbers of human skeletal remains and weapons have been dredged from the Meuse. As mentioned in Section 2.4, the remains can be interpreted as related to Caesar's destruction of the *Tencteri* and *Usipetes* in 55 BC. Most spectacular, however, is the battle-related find complex with large numbers of Roman coins and fragments of *militaria* excavated at Kalkriese in Lower Saxony. Most scholars accept that we are dealing here with the battlefield of Varus' disastrous defeat in AD 9, but such historical identifications are never absolutely certain and there is still some debate (Burmeister 2022; Kehne 2017, 2018). An alternative interpretation, that the

Kalkriese battlefield might be associated with one of the campaigns of Germanicus some years later, cannot be completely excluded at this stage.

Be that as it may, the research at Kalkriese has provided important insights into the phasing of activities related to the battle. It is generally known that the materials collected at a battlefield are not a simple reflection of combat activities but represent a complex sequence of events (Carman 2014; Roymans and Fernández-Götz 2018). The archaeological evidence is always heavily affected by post-battle activities, in particular the looting and cleaning of a battle site by the victorious party. At Kalkriese, detailed study of the Roman *militaria*, coins, and personal ornaments and their distribution patterns has been used for the spatial delimitation of the battle site and the identification of the zones of intense combat (Wilbers-Rost and Rost 2012, 2015). The excavations also produced evidence of the systematic collecting and processing of metal objects. Even more intriguing is the discovery in eight dispersed pits of a post-battle deposition of bones of fallen soldiers, mixed with some bones of *equidae* (Rost and Wilbers-Rost 2018). The bones were, with few exceptions, disarticulated and showed traces of exposure to the open air for several years. We can only speculate on who collected and buried the bones years after the battle. One scenario is to link the 'mass graves' with burial activities carried out by Germanicus during his historically documented visit to the Varus battlefield (Tac. *Ann.* 1.62).

Most archaeological research has focused on the study of the Roman military infrastructure, but some sites have also produced evidence for an initial urbanisation related to the establishment of a civic infrastructure in *Germania Magna* in the late Augustan period. In Haltern we can observe a gradual transformation of a military fortress into a civic centre. The best example, however, is the site of Waldgirmes in Hesse, where the remains of a newly founded municipal centre with public buildings, private houses, and a Roman-style spatial layout have been excavated (Becker and Rasbach 2015) (Figure 32). The building activities started just before 4 BC, which is the dendrochronologically established felling date of a tree used to line the walls of a well. The new town had a trapezoidal ground plan, two intersecting main streets, and in the centre a monumental *forum*. In its inner court there was a large gilded equestrian statue of Augustus, a key symbol of Roman power. The ceramics mainly consisted of imported Roman wares, but 20 per cent of the assemblage was handmade native-style pottery that clearly points to the presence in the town of an indigenous population. However, the town did not enjoy a long life. There is archaeological evidence for a violent destruction of the site: it was plundered and destroyed by fire, probably in association with the events of the Varus Battle. Of particular symbolic value was the cutting into pieces of the monumental equestrian statue of Augustus

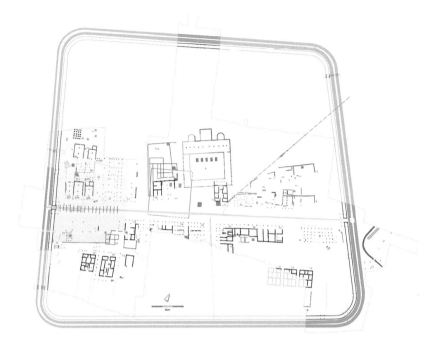

Figure 32 General plan of the Roman municipal centre of Waldgirmes. In the centre of the settlement in red was the *forum* with the foundation pits for a series of statues (© Römisch-Germanische Kommission, Frankfurt)

(Figure 33). Although there is evidence that some habitation continued in Waldgirmes after the Battle of the Teutoburg Forest, there is no doubt that the catastrophic defeat of AD 9 marked the end of the Roman initiatives to establish a municipal organisation east of the Rhine.

In the late Augustan period, we also see an initial exploitation of mineral resources by Rome in *Germania* east of the Rhine. Extraction of lead ore has been attested in the Sauerland area near Brilon (Hanel and Rothenhöfer 2005). A recent research project in the Lahn-Taunus area near Bad Ems has produced evidence of lead and silver ore mining. The presence of a Roman military camp from the Augustan period at the Alteburg suggests that the initiatives came from the Roman army, which may have exploited the mines using their own personnel or farmed out the exploitation to civil entrepreneurs, thereby providing logistical and technical support as well as security to the mining operations (Posluschny and Schade-Lindig 2019).

4.4 A Landscape of Trauma and Terror?

Compared to the significant scholarly investment in the investigation of the Roman military infrastructure, the impact of the wars on the indigenous

Figure 33 Gilded horse head of a monumental equestrian statue originally placed in the *forum* of Waldgirmes, but finally destroyed and thrown into a well shaft (© Hessenarchäologie, Wiesbaden)

populations has attracted little attention. However, based on the written accounts the impact must have been dramatic. The extensive reports of the campaigns of Caesar and Germanicus show us that the large-scale burning down and plundering of regions was the normal strategy against resistant enemy groups. Although we should take into account regional and temporal differences, there is no doubt that the losses must have been enormous in terms of human lives, enslaved persons, destroyed settlements, and stolen cattle. An analogy with the effects of the Thirty Years' War (1618–1648) suggests that most people did not necessarily fall by force of arms, but were the victims of starvation, disease outbreaks, large-scale deportation, and unorganised streams of refugees.

Lavan (2020) has recently made a comparative study of the textual and iconographic evidence for the destruction of populations and human landscapes in the Roman wars of conquest. He concludes that – although the imperial elite did not think that they engaged in mass destruction widely or indiscriminately – 'the empire's capacity to destroy was regularly evoked and celebrated. Mass destruction was authorised above all by the discourse of barbarism, especially the idea that some peoples were so recalcitrant or so untrustworthy that they were simply ungovernable. In such situations, annihilation seemed not only justifiable but necessary' (Lavan 2020, 202). The accounts of the campaigns of Caesar and Germanicus against Germanic groups provide ample examples for this (cf. Caesar, *BG* 4.4–15; 6.5–6; 8.24–25; Tac. *Ann.* 1.51.1; 2.21.2), as do the visual representations of Roman soldiers devastating indigenous settlements on the columns of Trajan and Marcus Aurelius in Rome (see Figure 3, Section 1.3).

Until now, archaeology has provided little insight into the direct effects of the Germanic Wars on indigenous populations and settlements. The number of excavated settlements is still small and does not allow broad generalisations. Moreover, there is the methodical problem of the frequently limited chronological resolution of settlement evidence, and the general problem that traces of organised violence are hardly detectable at the local level, especially when the ancient surfaces are not preserved. One of the few sites that has provided evidence for collective violence related to the Germanic Wars is the Late Iron Age *oppidum* at the Dünsberg in Hesse, Germany. An iron hobnail, Republican and Augustan bronze coins, as well as a concentration of lead sling bullets and other projectiles, may provide evidence for combat with a Roman armed force (Schulze-Forster 2002).

In theory, the study of regional fluctuations in habitation patterns in combination with palaeoenvironmental reconstructions of the vegetation history has the potential to identify periods of demographic regression corresponding to historically documented episodes of warfare (cf. Section 2.5). For the moment, however, high-quality regional fieldwork evidence that can be directly connected with the Germanic Wars is still rare, while the chronological resolution of pollen diagrams of peat layers is often too low to be helpful (cf. the regional studies by Folkers et al. 2018; Siegmüller 2018).

4.5 *Germania* as a Breeding Ground for Auxiliaries

A further theme that deserves special attention is the extensive military recruitment by Rome among Germanic groups. Rome made intensive use of Germanic auxiliary troops for its military campaigns in *Germania*. This practice served a dual purpose: it strengthened the Roman military potential while reducing the possible opposition from Germanic groups. Moreover, ethnic recruitment offered Rome an instrument for gaining the support of tribal elites by offering them the command of auxiliary war bands and admitting them to the clientele of Rome. Subjected tribes were forced to supply auxiliary forces as a kind of tribute, examples being the Frisians and the *Chauci*, and initially also the *Cherusci*. The result was that Germanic tribes were divided into pro- and anti-Roman coalitions, and individual positions of tribes or their leaders could change over the course of time. Even within a single tribe there could be serious dissension, an example being the *Cherusci* which had a dominant anti-Roman group led by Arminius but also a pro-Roman faction headed by Segestes. There was also an intensive ethnic recruitment among Germanic groups living on the west bank of the Rhine, in a zone that had been targeted for integration into the new province of *Germania*. Here many ethnic cohorts and *alae* are reported in the pre-Flavian period, which derived from irregular war bands from the time of the Germanic Wars, as is explicitly mentioned for the *Batavi* (Tac. *Hist.* 4.12).

Archaeology enables us to study the materiality of ethnic recruitment. Two categories of material are of special interest here: coins and Roman imports such as pottery and brooches. Regarding coins, a project in the Batavian region has produced an impressive database of Augustan bronze coinages found in indigenous settlements (Figure 34). The coins occur in almost every rural site and reflect a substantial coin influx into the rural community during the middle and late Augustan period (Roymans in prep.). This can best be interpreted as payment to Batavian auxiliaries, probably for buying food and drink during their service in the campaigning season. Military service created opportunities for both elite persons and common soldiers. The availability of Roman money gave members of auxiliary war bands already in the Augustan period the opportunity to buy a range of Roman commodities on the Roman military markets that they then brought back to their home settlements (Roymans 2011). *Terra sigillata* and different types of bronze brooches also frequently appear in rural contexts and may have been bought from merchants or craftsmen stationed in the Roman military centres. Concentrations of such early imports may indicate residences of pro-Roman leaders who operated as commanders of tribal war bands. A historical example is the Frisian Cruptorix, who had served in the Roman army in his earlier days and who by AD 29 resided in a '*villa*' in his homeland (Tac. *Ann.* 4.73).

4.6 Imperial Power, Human Mobility, and the Reshuffling of Tribal (Id)entities

Both historical and archaeological evidence suggest that the time of the Germanic Wars corresponded with a remarkable period of mobility of indigenous groups, which triggered a reshuffling of the tribal map resulting in new ethnogeneses and identity constructions of groups and individuals (Figure 35). There is often a direct relationship between such changes and Roman expansionist policy in the Germanic frontier zone, but if we adopt a long-term perspective, we also see some more structural patterns of mobility that connect to developments rooted in the Late Iron Age.

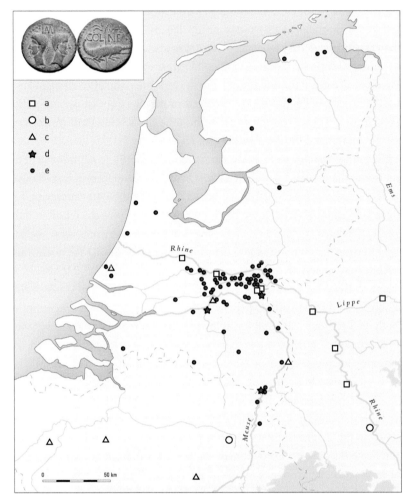

Figure 34 Distribution of bronze Nemausus I coins, massively used by the Roman army for payment of soldiers during the Germanic campaigns of Drusus. Only the coins from the Netherlands have been systematically mapped. a. Roman camp; b. Roman town; c. nucleated settlement; d. cult place; e. rural settlement (image: N. Roymans)

The written sources shed light on various forms of human mobility that are directly related to the Augustan project in *Germania*. Most prominent are the cyclical mobility of Germanic war bands serving on a seasonal basis in the Roman army and the large-scale reallocations of groups by the Roman authorities. But we should also take into account the enslavement of captives, and the occurrence of unorganised streams of refugees who tried to escape from the systematic destruction of regions. There are several examples of transfers of

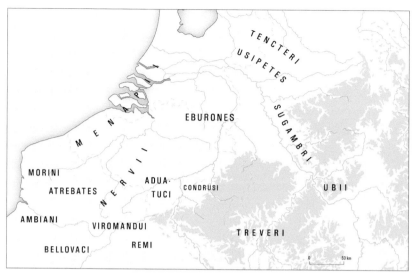

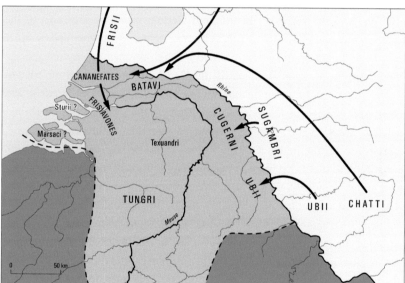

Figure 35 Above: tribal map of the Germanic frontier zone in the Caesarian period. Below: migratory movements across the Rhine in the Augustan/ Tiberian period (image: N. Roymans)

Germanic groups from the east to the west banks of the Rhine. In 8 BC Tiberius organised a forced deportation of defeated groups of *Sugambri* and *Suebi* to the Gallic bank of the Rhine (Tac. *Ann.* 12.39). The *Cugerni* in the area around the legionary camp of *Vetera* at modern Xanten are often thought to be descendants of these *Germani* resettled by Tiberius.

A somewhat different category are more voluntary moves of Germanic tribes which were allied to Rome. Examples are the resettlement of the *Ubii* and possibly also the *Batavi* to the west bank of the Rhine under the supervision of Agrippa in 20–19 BC, and the transfer to Gaul of the pro-Roman Cheruscan chief Segestes with his attendants and kinsmen in AD 15. However, recent archaeological case studies on the ethnogenesis of the *Batavi* warn us that written sources often present a heavily oversimplified picture of migrations: the *Batavi* were in fact a new creation based on the influx of several groups of settlers from different areas north and east of the Lower Rhine (Roymans and Habermehl 2023). The Batavian case shows us that intensive ethnic recruitment within a group could generate a sense of collective identity as a soldiering people (Roymans 2004).

Archaeology also draws our attention to a category of migrations that was not initiated by Rome. Studies of pottery and small metal objects point to a westward expansion of more eastern groups, a process that had already started in the Late Iron Age. In southern Germany and the area east of the Middle Rhine, groups with a La Tène-type material culture and a more hierarchical social organisation, marked by the presence of *oppida* and the use of coinage, were at least partly displaced by groups with an eastern material culture and a more heterarchical social structure. This process was further strengthened in the Augustan period by the reallocation of Rhine-Germanic groups with a strongly latènised material culture (*Ubii*, *Batavi*, *Sugambri*) to the Gallic bank of the Rhine. These demographic vacuums on the east bank of the Rhine were re-occupied by settlers of more eastern origin. Caesar in his comments on the Gallic Wars frequently mentions the mobility and westward migration of Germanic tribes, in particular the pressure of Ariovistus' Suebian groups (*BG* 1.31–33). Such passages have often been interpreted as imperialist rhetoric invoking a Germanic threat to Roman interests that politically justified further military interventions by Rome. Although this interpretation probably contains some truth, in this context we should also take into account the increasing archaeological evidence for a settlement of groups coming from the east. These new settlers probably played a key role in the formation of the new 'Rhine-Weser Germanic culture' in the early first century AD (Meyer 2013).

4.7 Why did Augustus' *Germania* Project Fail?

The Augustan *Germania* project is special since it represents one of the rare cases in which an imperial ambition of conquering an area and creating a new province failed. Tiberius' order to withdraw the troops to the Rhine in AD 16 marked the end of this ambition, although Rome continued its attempts to control the situation in *Germania* by diplomatic and military means, while archaeological evidence points to the importance of exchange relations in the next few centuries.

What were, however, the reasons for the failed conquest of *Germania*? A combination of factors played a role here. One reason seems to have been the extreme costs of the military operations in *Germania*, which were out of proportion in relation to the limited economic revenues expected from the new province. In the settlement sphere we see a strongly decentralised pattern and an absence of urbanised central places (Nüsse 2014), which would have been ideal military targets for the Roman army. *Germania* generally had low-productive agrarian regimes aimed at local autarky and lacked a system of regional surplus centralisation controlled by elites. This created huge logistic problems for Roman armies, which could not rely on local grain stores for their campaigns in *Germania*, but had to depend heavily on long supply lines from Gaul (Polak and Kooistra 2013).

The aforementioned factors, however, cannot be isolated from the specific social organisation of Germanic societies. Germanic tribes were often less hierarchical, relatively fluid political formations that were continuously subjected to processes of fission, fusion, and disintegration (Wolters 2017). The power of 'civil' elites was curtailed by tribal councils, in this way forming a system that was heavily based on 'power from below' mechanisms (Thurston and Fernández-Götz 2021). However, the domain of warfare was dominated by charismatic war leaders with a paramilitary following or *Gefolgschaft* recruited from different tribes; such war leaders often fell outside the control and violence monopoly of individual tribes. Rome's imperial expansion was normally based on a mixed use of both extreme violence and diplomacy. In *Germania*, however, there were limited possibilities to control peoples by means of targeted diplomacy. In contrast to Britain and Gaul, Rome failed to create client tribes with a stable, pro-Roman aristocracy in *Germania*. Given this situation, Rome's activities there were based on a disproportionate use of extreme violence, resulting in substantial financial costs for the military operations.

5 Beyond the Sea: The Roman Conquest of Britain

5.1 First Military Encounters: Caesar's Crossing of the Channel

Britain was the last of the regions analysed in this volume to be incorporated into the Roman Empire (cf. overview in Hingley 2022) (Figure 36). But although the actual conquest did not start until the Claudian invasion in AD 43, the first direct

Figure 36 Location of the main sites mentioned in Section 5 (authors)

military encounters go back to around a century earlier. Indeed, it was Julius Caesar who first crossed the Channel on two occasions (in 55 and 54 BC) in the context of his campaigns in Gaul (cf. Section 2), supposedly with the main aim of stopping the Britons from assisting their Gallic neighbours in their resistance against Rome. Moreover, from a Mediterranean perspective at that time Britain was still wrapped in an aura of mystery. Through his expeditions, Caesar was able to gather more information about the island and its inhabitants, as well as to reinforce his personal prestige with campaigns in distant, largely unknown lands on the edge of the known world.

Archaeology provides evidence for the close connections that existed between communities on both sides of the Channel before, during, and after the Gallic Wars (Lamb 2018). For example, the coastal site of Urville-Nacqueville – with its distinctive roundhouses and burials – has been dated from the late second to the early first centuries BC and interpreted as reflecting the settlement of some Britons in Normandy (Lefort et al. 2015). Evidence for intensive trade in the period immediately before the Gallic Wars can be found at places such as Hengistbury Head in southern England, where both Gallic and Roman material has been discovered, perhaps indicating the existence of an enclave of Gauls (Fitzpatrick 2001).

In addition, classical sources, particularly Caesar, mention the cross-Channel mobility of elite members. Prominent examples include Commius, a ruler of the northern Gallic *Atrebates* who changed sides during the course of the war and ended up as king in southern Britain, or the Gallic leaders of the *Bellovaci* who fled to Britain after their defeat in 57 BC. Archaeologically, a relatively recent discovery that illustrates the cross-Channel connections that existed in the context of the Gallic Wars is the burial of a warrior found at North Bersted in Sussex. The grave – which contained items such as a sword, a shield, and a remarkable helmet – has been interpreted as the interment of a northern Gallic elite member who fled to Britain in the 50s BC (Fitzpatrick 2023) (Figure 37). On the Channel Island of Jersey, an impressive hoard of nearly 70,000 coins – largely of the *Coriosolites* and probably produced during the time of the Gallic Wars – was discovered at Le Câtillon in 2012 (de Jersey 2019). The magnitude of the hoard is indicative of the scale of indigenous coin minting to pay soldiers during the years of the conflict – a phenomenon also observable in northern Gaul (cf. Section 2.6).

In his account about the two expeditions to Britain, Caesar provided details about aspects of local practices, such as the enduring use of chariots in battle by the Britons, and political affairs, including the names of some indigenous leaders such as Cassivellaunus. Caesar's first arrival took place in the summer of 55 BC, when he landed with an army of fewer than 10,000 troops. This first campaign only lasted for about a month and was limited to Kent. The following year Caesar returned to Britain, supposedly after a prince of the British tribe of the *Trinobantes* had asked him for help. This time Caesar arrived with a larger army – about 20,000 legionaries and cavalry – that campaigned in various parts of southeast England. He reports that the peace agreement following his military victory involved the taking of hostages and the payment of tributes to Rome by local tribes.

However, for a long time direct evidence for Caesar's short-lived military presence in Britain was virtually invisible in the archaeological record. This has now changed, primarily thanks to the work undertaken within the project 'In the Footsteps of Caesar' (Fitzpatrick 2018, 2019; Fitzpatrick and Haselgrove 2023). Thus, Caesar's landing site of 54 BC has been identified at Ebbsfleet in Kent, where a large ditch was first discovered in 2010. Subsequent fieldwork in

Figure 37 Idealised image of the North Bersted warrior (Copyright of The Novium Museum [a service provided by Chichester District Council].

2015–2017 uncovered further evidence of what seems to have been a defensive enclosure erected to protect Caesar's fleet of around 800 ships, a proposal that is consistent with the topographic clues provided in his writings. In terms of artefactual evidence, the most significant find was a metal object interpreted by the excavator as the tip of a Republican Roman *pilum* discovered in the defensive ditch.

5.2 Roman Influence between the Wars

Nearly one century passed between Caesar's departure in 54 BC and Claudius' arrival in AD 43. Unlike in Gaul, Caesar had no intention of leaving an occupying army in Britain; the prestige gained in Rome through his expeditions beyond the sea and the treaty relations established with some southern tribes seem to have satisfied his expectations. Augustus, for his part, considered invading the island on a few occasions, but none of the plans materialised due to other priorities and probably also the effectiveness of diplomacy. In any case, although no Roman troops remained in Britain after 54 BC, the influence of Rome was very much present, particularly in the southern part of the island. For example, Strabo (4.5.3) stated that some chieftains of the Britons had procured 'the friendship of Caesar Augustus by sending embassies and by paying court to him', and that they submitted 'so easily to heavy duties [. . .] that there is no need of garrisoning the island'. Contacts with the Roman world – including, decisively, with the recently conquered Gallic territories – flourished between the mid-first century BC and the mid-first century AD. This was especially the case in southeast Britain, as testified archaeologically by the arrival of objects such as amphorae and wine-drinking equipment. Some of these Roman imports were deposited in elaborate elite graves, such as the Welwyn burials (Champion 2016). That said, the use and deposition of foreign goods would have often been shaped by indigenous practices.

Among the most valuable sources for understanding Rome's influence on indigenous communities are the coins minted in Britain, some of which began to include legends in Latin and occasionally also images derived from the classical world (Creighton 2000). A small number of indigenous emissions even incorporated the Latin title 'REX'. Certain coins depicted leaders who bore names that at times can be correlated with notable individuals mentioned in written sources, such as Tincomarus, who might have spent some time as a diplomatic hostage in Rome (Figure 38). Among the Iron Age coins found in southern England are a number that include the inscription 'COMMIOS', which has been interpreted as referring to the aforementioned leader of the *Atrebates*. In fact, Commius seems to have started a dynasty after his move to Britain, being succeeded by Tincomarus. A key central place of the British *Atrebates* was the Late Iron Age *oppidum* of *Calleva* (Silchester), which exhibited ties with Belgic Gaul (Fulford et al. 2018).

It has been suggested that some of the British rulers mentioned in coins and/or written sources might have been recognised by Rome as client kings (Creighton 2000). Roman-friendly leaders would have seen the Empire as a potential ally in factional conflicts within and between British polities. During this period, we also

Figure 38 Gold coin of Tincomarus (© Ashmolean Museum,
University of Oxford)

witness the development of important seats of power, with prominent examples in
the south including *Camulodunum* (Colchester), *Verulamium* (St Albans), and
Calleva (Silchester) (Garland 2020) (Figure 39). The growing connections with
the Roman world are visible not only in terms of imported objects and local
coinage, but also in the archaeobotanical record. Thus, at *Calleva* it has been
documented that celery, coriander, and olives were already being imported and
consumed before the Claudian conquest (Lodwick 2014). However, it should be
noted that while Roman influence was particularly marked in southern Britain, it
was less pronounced in areas further to the north and west.

5.3 An Emperor's Ambition: The Claudian Invasion

In AD 43, the armies of Emperor Claudius arrived in Britain with the aim of
incorporating the island under direct Roman rule (Fields 2020). It is reported
that Verica, king of the *Atrebates*, had previously fled to Rome following
disputes in Britain. This provided Claudius with an excuse to intervene,
although his main motivations would have lain elsewhere. Indeed, the
Emperor had to strengthen his own position after his ascent to power, and an
exterior war of conquest would have represented an effective way of consolidating his leadership – a strategy also applied by many of his predecessors and
successors. High-resolution dating based on coins, milestones, and tree rings
suggests that preparations for the British campaign would have started at least
two years prior to the invasion, which indicates a carefully designed plan rather
than just a reaction to external events (Graafstal 2023).

Several legions under the command of Aulus Plautius landed in Britain in the
late summer of AD 43. The number of legions that initially arrived is still
unclear, with proposals ranging from three to four. Including the auxiliary
troops, the invading force would have probably encompassed around 30,000

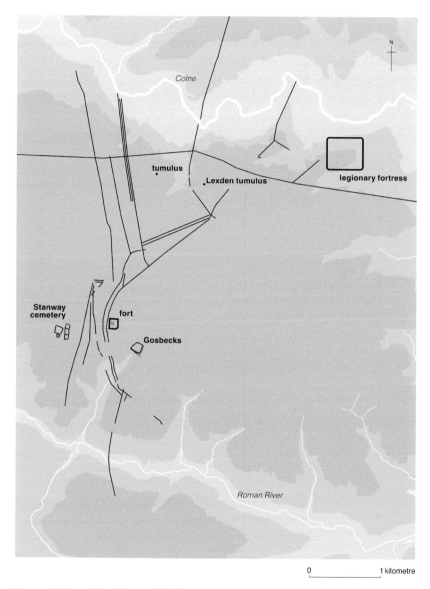

Figure 39 Late Iron Age and Early Roman *Camulodunum*, showing the features of the Iron Age *oppidum* and the location of the Roman fortress built during the conquest in AD 43–44 (after Hingley 2022)

to 40,000 men. While the exact landing place(s) of the troops has been the matter of long debate, with locations being proposed in Kent and Sussex (Sauer 2002), the discovery of two Roman military installations in close proximity to each other at Ebbsfleet and Richborough makes it more likely that the forces landed in Kent (Figure 40). Perhaps the Claudian invasion reused the location already employed by Caesar in 54 BC, as suggested by some mid-first century AD archaeological evidence at Ebbsfleet (Fitzpatrick 2019). Due to its strategic position, Richborough developed into a major gateway for the arrival of supplies for the Roman military (Millett and Wilmott 2003).

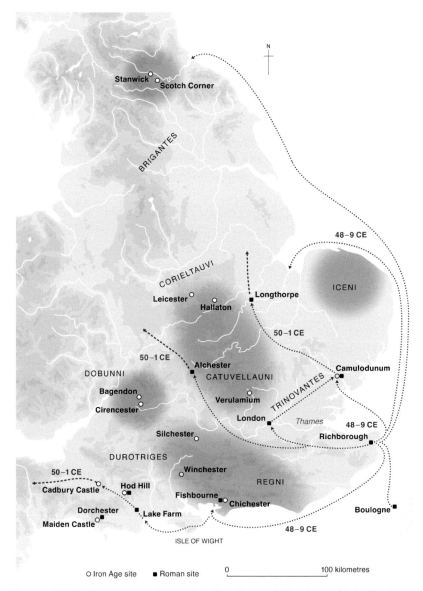

Figure 40 The Roman invasion under Claudius and Plautius, with indication of places, peoples, and campaign routes on land and sea; the darker areas indicate likely friendly kingdoms in the Claudian period (after Hingley 2022)

The Roman army rapidly established control over large parts of southeast England, winning important battles on the rivers Medway and Thames and defeating indigenous leaders such as Caratacus and Togodumnus. Emperor Claudius himself only came to Britain for slightly over two weeks, long enough to accept the surrender of several kings at *Camulodunum*. Several 'friendly kingdoms' were soon established, showing that the Roman conquest was the result of combining military power with an effective diplomacy that included collaboration with pro-Roman native rulers. Examples of the latter were Togidubnus, named in an inscription from Chichester as Tiberius Claudius Togidubnus, and perhaps also the individual in the rich burial at Folly Lane near *Verulamium* (Hingley 2022).

That the influence of Rome already extended far beyond the territories of the actual military conquest is exemplified by the mention of a king of the *Orcades* (Orkney Islands) as one of the British rulers that visited Claudius in AD 43. In this sense, the discovery of a Haltern type 70 Roman amphora at the Broch of Gurness in Mainland Orkney testifies that there were contacts with the far north even before the time of Agricola's campaigns (Fitzpatrick 1989). In northern England, the pro-Roman Cartimandua was the queen of the *Brigantes* in the decades following the Claudian invasion. Stanwick (Yorkshire) probably acted as the main power base of this client kingdom, as suggested by the large dimensions of the *oppidum* there (ca. 270 ha) and the arrival of abundant Roman objects including tableware and glass vessels (Haselgrove 2016). However, the complexity of internal politics and the tensions arising within and between communities are exemplified by the anti-Roman faction that was led by Cartimandua's consort Venutius, first in the AD 50s and then again in AD 69.

5.4 Tracing the Legions in Southern Britain

Direct archaeological evidence for the Claudian conquest of southern Britain is often ambiguous and contested. For example, there are numerous Roman camps (Jones 2012), but establishing their chronology is frequently challenging and it is sometimes difficult to discern if certain sites date to the Claudian or the Neronian period. Nonetheless, progress has been made in recent years, for instance through extensive geophysical surveys such as the one undertaken at the Roman fort at Lake Farm (Stewart et al. 2020), which would have been a major military base in the territory of the *Durotriges* (see also Sauer et al. 2000). In the area of the *Catuvellauni*, a possible battle has been recently identified at Windridge Farm near St Albans (Reid et al. 2022). Over 100 Roman lead sling bullets have been found widely dispersed at the

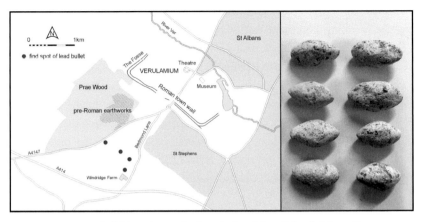

Figure 41 Windridge Farm. Left: relationship of the fields to Roman
Verulamium; the red dots mark the find spots of four bullets recorded on the
Portable Antiquities Scheme's database. Right: selection of bullets
(after Reid et al. 2022)

site since the 1970s, but they were initially interpreted as coming from
a plough-disturbed hoard. However, new research, which includes
a comparison with other sling bullet finds from Britain as well as isotopic
analyses, makes it much more plausible that they represent evidence of
a significant conflict episode linked to the Roman conquest of the island
(Figure 41). The authors suggest that the Roman projectiles most likely
relate to a Claudian period event, although a link with other historical
scenarios dating to the early Roman presence cannot be completely
discarded.

   In addition, there are also several indigenous hillforts that deserve special
attention in relation to the early stages of the conquest. This is the case for some
sites located in the territory attributed to the *Durotriges*, which was conquered
by the commander of the *Legio II Augusta* and future Emperor Vespasian. One
of the most interesting examples is Hod Hill, a large hillfort enclosing 22 ha in
which several Roman ballista bolts were discovered among some of the indigenous houses. These projectiles and the fact that a rectangular Roman fort was
built in the mid-40s AD inside the ramparts of the Iron Age hillfort suggest an
attack and subsequent occupation of Hod Hill by the Roman army (Richmond
1968) (Figure 42). Another interesting site is Cadbury Castle, where weaponry
of both indigenous and Roman military type as well as human remains with
traces of injuries indicate a violent attack on the hillfort; evidence of a post-
conquest Roman military occupation is also present in the form of barracks
(Barrett et al. 2000).

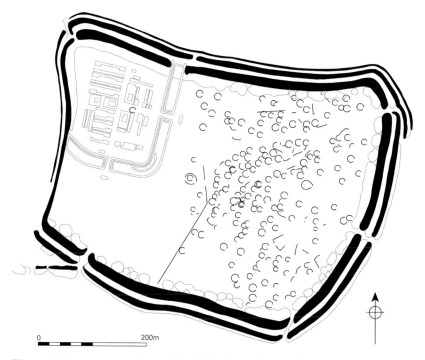

Figure 42 Interpretive plan of Hod Hill, including the Roman camp that was built in one of the corners (after Sharples 2014)

In any case, the hillfort that has generated more debate since Wheeler's excavations in the 1930s is Maiden Castle, which has one of the most spectacular multivallate fortification systems in Europe, enclosing an area of 19 ha. Wheeler's interpretation of the so-called war cemetery as including the graves of indigenous people that would have died during the Roman assault of the hillfort was later questioned. A reassessment of the data indicates that the traces of injuries, while abundant, are unlikely to reflect a single episode of warfare (Redfern 2011). Although the possibility of some sort of Roman military engagement at Maiden Castle should not be disregarded to the extent proposed in some recent work (Russell 2019), at least some of the burials seem to include evidence for Iron Age violence taking place prior to the Roman conquest.

5.5 The Warrior Queen: Boudica's Revolt

After the initial conquest campaigns, the next major historical event reported in the sources was the uprising that took place in AD 60/61 under the direction of one of the most iconic figures in British history: Boudica, queen of the *Iceni* (Gillespie 2018; Hingley and Unwin 2005). This 'warrior queen' is regarded as an example of resistance against the invader and – together with the pro-Roman Cartimandua – as a prime exponent of the important political role that some women performed in Iron Age societies. The significance awarded to Boudica in the Modern Era is exemplified by the monumental bronze sculptural group that was erected next to the Houses of Parliament in London.

Boudica's uprising started after the abuses that she, her two daughters, and other leading figures of the tribe suffered from the Romans following the death of her husband, the client king Prasutagus who had reigned over the *Iceni* of present-day East Anglia. While personal grievances certainly played a role in the start of the revolt, the substantial – although by no means universal – support that it gained among various indigenous groups was fuelled by deeper discontent with the Roman domination. Religious factors might have also played a role. In the years following Plautius' departure in AD 47, much of the Roman military activity focused on campaigns in Wales, where the invaders encountered some serious resistance by groups such as the *Silures* and the *Ordovices*. In AD 60, the Romans attacked the island of *Mona* (Anglesey) in north Wales, regarded as a major centre of the druids. It has been proposed that Boudica's revolt could have been at least partly a response to the Roman campaign against this place of supra-regional religious significance (Aldhouse-Green 2006).

Be that as it may, Boudica's forces launched a devastating attack against the Roman colony of *Camulodunum* (*Colonia Claudia Victricensis*), the main centre of Roman power in Britain since the Claudian conquest, which was razed to the ground. *Londinium* (London) and *Verulamium* were also destroyed, which means that the three most important towns of Roman Britain suffered a dramatic fate (Tac. *Ann.* 14.32–33) (Figure 43). We have archaeological evidence for these destructions in the form of fire debris that can be connected with the historical events of AD 60/61 at *Camulodunum*, *Londinium*, and *Verulamium* (Hingley 2018; Wallace 2016). The burnt deposits confirm the written reports about the destruction of the towns, although the archaeological evidence also indicates that the urban centres started to be rebuilt shortly afterwards.

Despite their initial successes, Boudica's troops were decisively defeated by the Roman commander Suetonius Paulinus at a battle in southern Britain whose exact location has not yet been confirmed archaeologically. In this context, it should also be highlighted that the rebellion was not joined by all indigenous groups; powerful leaders such as Togidubnus and Cartimandua stayed loyal to Rome, a fact that certainly contributed to the suppression of the uprising. The Roman reprisal was merciless: Tacitus (*Ann.* 14.37) estimated that around 80,000 Britons fell during the battle (including non-combatants), and while

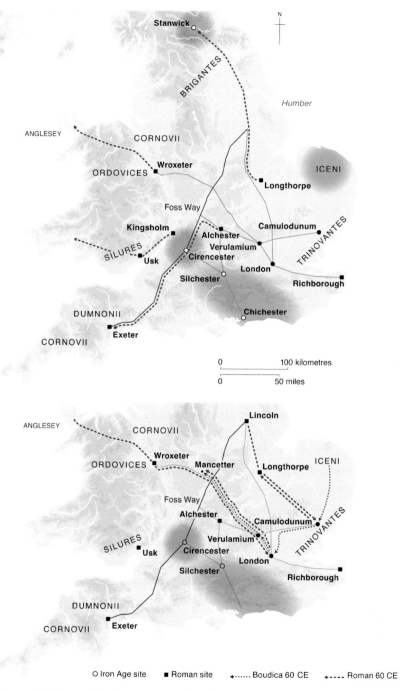

Figure 43 Above: The Roman campaigns between AD 54 and AD 60, showing forts and towns. Below: The events of the Boudican revolt (after Hingley 2022)

these figures might be exaggerated, many others would have died in subsequent punitive actions by the Roman army and as a result of food shortages. While ultimately unsuccessful, the story of Boudica's rebellion is one of the most prominent examples of the various uprisings that arose against Roman domination in the years and decades following the initial military conquests – from Iberia to Britain and from Gaul to *Germania* and beyond.

5.6 Into the North: Agricola's Campaigns

A renewed push in Rome's attempts to complete the conquest of Britain started with the appointment of Gnaeus Julius Agricola as new provincial governor in AD 77. His actions are best known through the writings of his son-in-law, Tacitus, who provided a valuable but biased and sometimes imprecise account of these activities. Agricola directed a number of military campaigns to conquer the populations that still resisted Roman control, starting with a brutal repression against the *Ordovices* in Wales. He then moved his attention to the north, which became his main theatre of operations. Archaeology, in any case, has demonstrated that there had already been Roman military activity in northern England pre-dating Agricola's campaigns, as testified by the early fort at Carlisle, which has provided a dendrochronological date of AD 72 (McCarthy 2018). This site was probably connected to the campaign led by Cerialis against the *Brigantes* after they had driven out the pro-Roman queen Cartimandua in AD 69.

Agricola's campaigns into Scotland seem to have followed two main land routes, which would have run from the areas of the forts at Corbridge and Carlisle, respectively, towards the north. There are also references to the role of the fleet. Besides the information provided by Tacitus, much of our knowledge of Agricola's operations is based on the material record provided by Roman military structures identified in Scotland. This region has one of the largest corpora of known Roman fortifications from the first centuries AD in the whole of Europe (Breeze 2006; Jones 2011) (Figure 44). However, establishing reliable chronologies that connect specific sites with campaigns mentioned in written sources is often challenging, since some sites were used at various points in time and in addition many have been identified only through non-invasive archaeological techniques such as aerial photography.

Among the most comprehensively excavated examples is the Roman fort at Elginhaugh near Edinburgh, whose foundation can be dated to the early stages of Agricola's operations in Scotland. The extensive excavations offer important insights into the structure of a timber-built auxiliary fort of the period (Hanson 2007). In southwest Scotland, a significant recent discovery is the identification of a Flavian period Roman marching camp in Ayr, which offers hitherto unknown

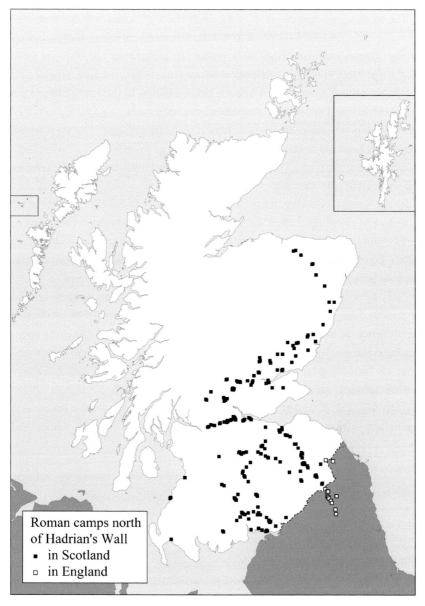

Figure 44 Roman camps north of Hadrian's Wall (image: R. Jones)

clues about operations in this region (Arabaolaza 2019). In Aberdeenshire we can highlight the excavations carried out at a large Roman camp of over 40 ha at Kintore (Cook and Dunbar 2008), as well as the 90 Roman bread ovens that have been uncovered at Milltimber (Dingwall and Shepherd 2018). In both cases, the sites are likely to be related to Agricola's campaigns in the northeast.

The most significant military event described by Tacitus was the Battle of *Mons Graupius*, which took place in AD 83. The numbers of reported casualties on the Roman side (less than 400) versus the indigenous (10,000) are most likely distorted, but it is reasonable to assume that the battle represented a substantial Roman victory. While the exact location of the battle has not yet been corroborated and several proposals have been made, it is usually assumed that it took place somewhere in the region of Aberdeenshire. The most recent suggestion has been to locate the battle at the Hill of Tillymorgan, near the large Roman camp of Ythan Wells (Reid 2023), a proposal that is still pending archaeological confirmation.

In the years following the victory at *Mons Graupius* the Roman army withdrew to positions further south, leaving the previously established line of fortifications known as the Gask Ridge abandoned (Woolliscroft and Hoffmann 2006). Despite various later invasions and attempts to establish Roman dominion over parts of Scotland, the conquest of Britain remained incomplete. Major military activity took place again in the Antonine and Severan periods, only to be followed by renewed withdrawals. Related to the period of the Antonine reoccupation of southern Scotland in the mid-second century AD is the spectacular evidence from Burnswark Hill, which includes two Roman camps and over 700 lead sling bullets, which can be convincingly linked with a massive Roman assault on the indigenous hillfort (Reid and Nicholson 2019) (Figure 45). On the other hand, the cruelty of the early third century AD campaigns is exemplified by a quote from Cassius Dio (77.15), who stated

Figure 45 Burnswark hillfort, with Roman military camp at its foot
(photo: J. Reid)

that Septimius Severus instructed his troops to: 'Let no one escape sheer destruction, no one our hands, not even the babe in the womb of the mother'.

However, all of these conquest attempts remained ephemeral. The reasons for Rome's failed conquest of Scotland have been much debated (Breeze 1988). While in the short-term it is likely that factors such as the need for troops elsewhere in the Empire might explain certain outcomes, in the longer-term other factors of a more structural nature need to be taken into account (Fernández-Götz and Roymans in press). Similar to what has been discussed for *Germania* (Section 4), the social organisation of indigenous Iron Age communities would have played an important role, a topic to which we will return in Section 6.3. Scotland remained very much a 'frontier country' (Breeze 2006), with the nature of the Roman presence being a primarily military one. Thus, the high number of military installations contrasts with the absence of Roman town foundations or villas north of Hadrian's Wall, which indicates that the process of power consolidation never went as far as to establish the civil network that could be expected in a province.

6 Conclusion

6.1 On Sources and Methods

The case studies presented in this volume have showcased multiple ways in which archaeology can contribute to a better understanding of the Roman conquest. However, when drawing conclusions about the characteristics of the military conflicts and their impact on indigenous societies, it is important to take into account the uneven nature of the literary and archaeological data available for the various regions. For example, certain military campaigns are mentioned very briefly in written sources in no more than one or two sentences, which can potentially conceal cases of atrocities that become explicit in more detailed accounts such as Caesar's *Commentarii* – absence of evidence does not therefore necessarily imply evidence of absence. Regarding the archaeological evidence, rarely do we have simultaneous access to extensive data coming from a wide range of sources, which means that in some regions we might be able to say more about demography, in others about military installations, and in others about the extraction of wealth, to name just some examples.

For instance, in the Lower Rhine region the abundant and relatively well-dated settlement evidence often enables inferences to be made about the demographic impact of the conquest on the scale of generations (Section 2.5), but at the same time the number of known Roman temporary camps is still relatively small. The opposite is true for Scotland, where over 250 temporary camps are known but very few indigenous settlements have chronological sequences that can be correlated, even tentatively, with specific periods of Roman military activity (Section 5.6). On the other hand, indigenous coinage production offers interesting clues about wealth extraction and/or power relations in parts of Gaul and southern Britain (Sections 2.6 and 5.2), but such evidence is absent in areas like northern Spain. This latter region, in turn, has provided some of the most spectacular examples of Roman attacks on indigenous *oppida* (Section 3.4). While some of these data disparities might be mitigated, at least partly, in the future thanks to new research (for example, through an increasing number and refined modelling of radiocarbon dates, cf. Fernández-Götz et al. 2022), we need to accept that the type of insights that we can gain will continue to vary depending on the nature of the case studies. Thus, different types of sources require specific analytical and interpretative methodologies for their study (Sections 1.3–1.5).

As we have seen, archaeology can sometimes corroborate information provided in written sources, for example regarding the substantial demographic impact of the conquest in the so-called Germanic frontier zone (Section 2.5), the brutality of the actions against the *Cantabri* and *Astures* (Sections 3.4–3.6), the intensive recruitment of auxiliary troops among some Germanic groups (Section 4.5), and the destruction horizons caused by Boudica's revolt in southern England (Section 5.5). But in all these cases archaeology also adds some important nuances, showing that reality was usually much more complex than what was reported by ancient authors and/or revealing some aspects not directly mentioned in written sources. In this sense, we can observe differences in settlement trajectories between the five test regions analysed in northeast Gaul, identify some of the main types of weapons and assault tactics employed by the Roman army in the Cantabrian Mountains, recognise that the ethnogenesis of the *Batavi* was a complex process involving the influx of multiple groups of settlers, and assess the temporalities of town rebuilding after the Boudican destruction. There are also instances in which archaeology can reveal conflict scenarios that were previously completely unknown, as in the case of the siege of the *oppidum* of Cerro de Castarreño (Section 3.3). Finally, in some cases archaeology contradicts the information contained in written sources: for example, the abundant references by classical writers to dense forests and marshes in Britain seem to frequently respond to literary *topoi* that do not necessarily conform to the picture provided by the palaeoenvironmental evidence (Breeze 2019).

6.2 Roman Violence beyond the Battlefield

Analysing the process of conquest confronts us with the wider topic of the 'dark sides' of imperialism (cf. Elkins 2022; Mignolo 2011), which in the case of the Roman Empire included cases of slaughtering, mass enslavement, and even genocide (Fernández-Götz et al. 2020; Padilla Peralta 2020; Raaflaub 2021; Shaw in press; Taylor 2023). Several examples from Western and Central Europe have been mentioned in the preceding sections and similar cases can be found in many other regions that were violently incorporated into the Roman Empire, such as *Dacia* and *Judea*. But violence is not only a physical phenomenon, since it can also include other dimensions such as structural and cultural violence (Galtung 1990; Scheper-Hughes and Bourgois 2004; Žižek 2008). Violence, from this perspective, did not necessarily end with the individual Roman military conquests, but often extended to many spheres of life in the aftermath of the campaigns: from dispossessing people of their lands in order to make room for colonial settlers to a wide range of changes in the political, economic, and religious realms. These could encompass, for instance, the imposition of a new ideology, the banning of previous cultural practices, and the sharpening of social inequalities. The Roman conquest caused changes in local power relations, for example by promoting and rewarding kings and aristocrats who collaborated with the Empire to the detriment of other social groups. Symbolic violence was materialised, among other examples, in the abundant iconography that celebrated victories over foreign 'barbarians', both in the city of Rome itself (e.g. Trajan's Column) and in the conquered territories (e.g. the Bridgeness Distance Slab in Scotland) (Figure 46).

The Roman conquest would have generated phenomena of ontological insecurity, starting with the profound mark left by military defeat on the self-esteem and self-perception of the vanquished. Following Bourdieu (1977, 1990), when a way of life is subject to doubt or threatened by another, the *doxa* – i.e. the set of beliefs and social practices that are considered normal in a certain social context – is fractured and undergoes a transformation; this is precisely what would have very frequently happened during the processes of integration into the Roman world. In addition, it is well known that the repercussions of wars not only affect the people who directly suffer them, but very often percolate for generations. Thus, trauma and memory studies have shown how experiences of violence and displacement can continue to shape – consciously or unconsciously – the memories and experiences of descendants, as exemplified by the ongoing effects of disruptive episodes such as the Spanish Civil War or the Yugoslav Wars up to the present (Danieli 1998; González-Ruibal and Moshenska 2015). While exploring in more detail these other dimensions of violence during and after the Roman wars of conquest would exceed the scope of this Element volume, they should at least be taken into consideration when analysing the processes of integration into the Roman world.

In a recent article, Padilla Peralta (2020) has explored the concept of epistemicide, applying it to the Roman world. He argues that an astounding

Figure 46 The Bridgeness Roman distance slab, which commemorates the building of the Antonine Wall's eastern end and includes a depiction of a Roman officer riding down local warriors (© National Museums Scotland)

loss of epistemic diversity –traceable along multiple vectors, from ecological upheaval to mass enslavement – was engineered by Rome throughout the Mediterranean. His analysis is inspired by the work of postcolonial theorist Santos, according to whom: 'Colonial domination involves the deliberate destruction of other cultures. The destruction of knowledge (besides the genocide of indigenous people) is what I call epistemicide: the destruction of the knowledge and cultures of these populations, of their memories and ancestral links and their manner of relating to others and to nature' (Santos 2016: 18). The regions analysed in this volume offer some revealing examples for these types of phenomena in the post-conquest period. Thus, the banning of druidic practices by various Roman emperors can be regarded as an intentional obliteration of important elements of culture and memory, given the central role that the druids played among the societies of Gaul and Britain (Aldhouse-Green 2010; Webster 1999). Ecological upheaval, for its part, can be clearly observed in cases such as the mines of Las Médulas in northwestern Spain, located in the conquered territory of the *Astures* (Sánchez-Palencia 2000) (Figure 47). The exploitation of these mines illustrates two sides of the

Figure 47 Aerial view of the gold mining area of Las Médulas (photo: C. Frayle, public domain)

same coin. On the one hand, it became the largest open-pit gold mining area in the Roman Empire and a place of remarkable engineering achievements. But on the other hand, Las Médulas represents a prime case of landscape destruction and environmental impact, as reflected in high levels of lead pollution (Hillman et al. 2017). More broadly, data from peatlands, lakes, and ice cores indicate that the unprecedented scale of mining activity across the Roman Empire resulted in pollution of the environment at a hemispheric scale (Silva-Sánchez and Armada 2023).

The example of Las Médulas puts at the forefront the economic dimension of the conquest campaigns and their aftermath: mass enslavement and looting during the military campaigns were soon followed by new taxation rules and the large-scale extraction of material wealth through mining and other activities in the post-conquest period. Other phenomena such as the direct military exploitation of conquered groups as sources of auxiliary troops also need to be taken into account. All these vectors of exploitation were part of the 'predatory regime' that, as outlined in Section 1.6, characterised the political economy of Late Republican and Early Imperial Rome (Fernández-Götz et al. 2020). Having said this, regional differences and transformations over time need to be acknowledged (Mattingly 2011), in conjunction with factors of a more ideological nature. Among the latter are the considerations made in Section 5 in relation to the aura of mystery that surrounded the lands of

Britannia, which would have acted as one of the motivations for the Caesarian and Claudian campaigns beyond the sea (Hingley 2022).

6.3 Failed Conquests: The Importance of the Pre-Roman Background

While most of the regions discussed in this volume ended up being annexed into the Roman Empire, there were some exceptions, most notably *Germania* east of the Rhine and Britain north of Hadrian's Wall. In both cases, we can speak of 'failed' conquests, i.e. of regions that escaped effective control over the long-term despite various attempts to incorporate them into the Roman state. We know that, at least initially, the aim was to complete the conquest of both territories: Augustus' ambition was to transform the area between Rhine and Elbe into a regular Roman province, and in the case of Britain the initial idea was to conquer the entire island. The question of why the conquests stopped when and where they did has generated considerable debate, with explanations traditionally tending to put the emphasis on the Roman perspective. The main, sometimes interconnected, reasons cited by authors include the decisions of specific Roman emperors and generals, the need for troops elsewhere in the Empire, and the lack of interest in territories that were supposedly regarded as not economically worthwhile. When the indigenous side of the story is considered, it is generally focused on highlighting the actions of single individuals such as Arminius.

Many of the aforementioned factors could have indeed played an important role, particularly in the short-term. Thus, it is quite likely that the need for troops in the Danube region against the Dacians was a key factor in Rome's withdrawal from most of Scotland in the years following the victory at the Battle of *Mons Graupius* (Breeze 1988), and there is little doubt that the defeat at the Battle of the Teutoburg Forest represented a major turning point that halted the Augustan expansion into *Germania* (Wells 2003). However, if we adopt a longer-term perspective, other factors of a more structural nature need to be included in the equation. In particular, we want to put the focus on the importance of the indigenous background, arguing that the more heterarchical, decentralised, and fluid nature of power distribution among the societies of *Germania* and Scotland was one of the main reasons, if not the principal one, that explains why Rome was ultimately unable to incorporate them effectively into the Empire (for a more in-depth discussion cf. Fernández-Götz and Roymans in press).

Adopting a macro-scale perspective, it has been noted that in Western and Central Europe the limits of the Roman expansion largely coincided with the distribution of Late Iron Age *oppida* (Figure 48). This suggests that it was easier

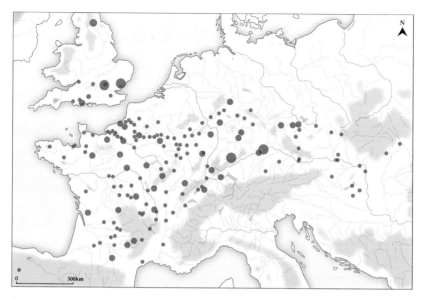

Figure 48 Distribution of fortified *oppida* in temperate Europe, second–first centuries BC (after Fernández-Götz 2018, based on data from www.oppida.org/, with additions)

for Rome to incorporate on a permanent basis regions in which societies were already organised around large central places, often of an urban character, than others where these structures were lacking. As indicated by Snodgrass (2017: 116): 'the spread of pre-Roman urbanization did not merely prepare the path for the fully fledged version that the Romans brought, but decisively influenced its success or failure'.

This should not be surprising: throughout history, for many empires it has been quicker and easier to establish control over communities that already had marked social hierarchies and were organised around urban centres than over tribal groups of a more dispersed and fluid character. A prime example is represented by the Spanish conquest of the Americas, in which conquistadors took control over the hierarchically organised Aztec and Inca states relatively quickly, whereas against the Mapuche populations of south-central Chile and southwestern Argentina they struggled for centuries. The Arauco War encompassed a series of conflicts over several generations in which the Mapuche opposed Spanish domination, with substantial costs for both sides (Cruz 2010).

Returning to the Roman Empire, the main lesson from the Germanic and Scottish case studies is that Roman imperial conquest was not inevitable, nor was it one-sidedly culturally or militarily determined. The characteristics of the indigenous populations, in combination with other factors such as geography and climate, could sometimes define the limits of Roman expansion. The social organisation of communities in *Germania* and Scotland, with their changing coalitions, flexible hierarchies, and largely dispersed settlement patterns, made it difficult for the Roman military command to effectively control the situation. This hindered the establishment of a provincial organisation in these territories, even in the aftermath of military victories: winning battles and controlling the population did not necessarily go hand in hand. This often frustrated the Roman generals, leading to the use of mass violence and scorched-earth tactics. The disproportionate use of extreme violence by Roman forces and the relatively fluid and less hierarchical nature of indigenous political formations, which made them more difficult to control, resulted in vast expenditures for Rome. This combination of factors in the end led to a failure in conquering the territories beyond the Rhine and Hadrian's Wall.

6.4 Reclaiming the Conquered, Rebalancing the View

As indicated in the subtitle of this Element, one of our aims has been to 'reclaim' the conquered through the analysis of some of the material evidence associated with the most brutal sides of Roman imperialism. The large-scale destruction of northern Spanish *oppida*, such as Monte Bernorio and La Loma, or the significant disruption in settlement trajectories that can be observed in the Lower Rhine region remind us that the process of integration into the Roman world was an imperialist act that ultimately brought with it the death and loss of liberty of millions of people. While there were multiple pathways for integration into the Roman world and not all communities would have suffered traumatic consequences, for many people Rome was, in the words of Shaw (in press), 'the exterminating angel'.

However, the aforementioned considerations should not lead us to view indigenous persons and groups merely as passive victims of imperial aggression. As already mentioned and exemplified throughout the volume, indigenous communities constituted neither homogenous nor static groups, but rather had their own agency and presented considerable diversity and dynamism. Pro- and anti-Roman factions often existed within the same tribes or even the same families, as exemplified by the cases of Diviciacus and Dumnorix among the *Aedui* or Cingetorix and Indutiomarus among the *Treveri*. Agendas and strategies in relation to Rome could also change over time, with persons and communities switching sides according to the circumstances. Cases of fierce resistance against Rome undoubtedly existed, and the abundant evidence for mass-murder and destruction that we encounter in both textual and archaeological sources should not be sanitised. But equally, we find many instances of cooperation, exchange, and hybridisation. The case of the 'friendly kingdoms' in Britain (Section 5) underlines the importance of negotiation and the active incorporation of (some) local elites into the new power networks. Thus, integration into the Roman world was a complex and multifaceted process that led to diverse outcomes in the provinces (Mattingly 2011; Revell 2009). Highlighting this complexity is also part of 'reclaiming' the conquered.

We should also be wary of portraying an idealised picture of Iron Age communities before the conquest period. Violence was already a common feature in pre-Roman Iron Age societies (Fernández-Götz and Arnold 2019), including occasional cases of massacres such as at the site of La Hoya in northern Spain (Fernández-Crespo et al. 2020). Slavery was also not alien to Iron Age temperate Europe, both internally and for export to the Mediterranean markets (Mata 2019; Redfern 2020). What Rome did during the wars of conquest in Western and Central Europe was, however, to bring violence and enslavement to another level, at least in terms of scale. As pointed out by Reid (2023: 68): 'Roman cruelty was, in its individual horrors, no more extreme than any other culture of its time, but it was more systematised and persistent, and was orchestrated on an unimaginable scale'.

All empires, ancient and modern, have both 'bright' and 'dark' sides, which are fundamentally intertwined. Thus, when we see the monumentality of the ancient city of Rome, the villa landscapes that proliferated across the Empire, and the richness of the material culture used by the upper classes, we should keep in mind that – beyond the apparent splendour – what we observe was the product of a system largely based on the spoils of conquest, the exploitation of the annexed territories, and a highly unequal society in which slaves represented a fundamental part of the workforce. In this Element volume, we have made a conscious choice to focus on some of the 'darkest' aspects of Roman history: the conquest of new populations by the extraordinarily powerful and efficient, but often extremely brutal, military machine of Late Republican and Early Imperial Rome. With this approach, we aim to highlight the substantial contribution that archaeology can make to the study of the Roman expansion, and at the same time reclaim the memory of those 'left behind' by the conquest process. By paying more attention to the 'dark sides' of imperialism, we intend to contribute to current efforts to decolonise Roman studies and produce a more inclusive picture of the past. This is an ongoing task, which aims to give voice to the voiceless by uncovering their stories of suffering and oppression – not in order to demonise ancient Rome, but with the aim of rebalancing our narratives (Gardner 2020). A holistic history needs to encompass victors and vanquished, winners and losers, and all those people who cannot easily be assigned to one of these two poles, and who merely tried to survive and adapt as best they could to the changing times through which they lived.

References

Classical Sources

Appian (2019). *Roman History*, B. McGing (ed. and trans.). Loeb Classical Library, Cambridge, MA.

Augustus (2009). *Res Gestae Divi Augusti*, A. Cooley (ed. and trans.). Cambridge University Press, Cambridge.

Caesar (1917). *The Gallic War*, H. J. Edwards (trans.). Loeb Classical Library, Cambridge, MA.

Cassius Dio (1917). *Roman History, Books LI-LV*, E. Cary (trans.). Loeb Classical Library, Cambridge, MA.

Florus (1984). *Epitome of Roman History*, E. S. Forster (trans.). Loeb Classical Library, Cambridge, MA.

Plutarch (1919). *Lives, Volume VII: Demosthenes and Cicero. Alexander and Caesar*, B. Perrin (trans.). Loeb Classical Library, Cambridge, MA.

Strabo (1923). *Geography, Books 3–5*, H. L. Jones (trans.). Loeb Classical Library, Cambridge, MA.

Suetonius (1998). *Lives of the Caesars, Vol. 1*, J.C. Rolfe (trans.). Loeb Classical Library, Cambridge, MA.

Tacitus (1931). *The Histories, Books IV-V*, C. H. Moore (trans.). Loeb Classical Library, Cambridge, MA.

Tacitus (1937). *The Annals*, J. Jackson (trans.). Loeb Classical Library, Cambridge, MA.

Modern Sources

Aldhouse-Green, M. (2006). *Boudica Britannia*. Pearson, Harlow.

Aldhouse-Green, M. (2010). *Caesar's Druids*. Yale University Press, New Haven, CT.

Alföldy, G. (2000). Das neue Edikt des Augustus aus El Bierzo in Hispanien. *Zeitschrift für Papyrologie und Epigraphik* 131: 177–205.

Amela, L. (2013–14). La conquista del norte peninsular. Primeros tanteos según las fuentes literarias. *Hispania Antiqua* XXXVII–XXXVIII: 69–84.

Arabaolaza, I. (2019). A Roman marching camp in Ayr. *Britannia* 50: 330–349.

Badian, E. (1968). *Roman Imperialism in the Late Republic*. Cornell University Press, Ithaca, NY.

Ball, J. (2014). Small finds and Roman battlefields: The process and impact of post-battle looting. In H. Platts, J. Pearce, C. Barron, J. Lundock and J. Yoo (eds.), *TRAC 2013: Proceedings of the 23rd Annual Theoretical Roman Archaeology Conference*. Oxbow, Oxford: 90–104.

Barrandon, N. (2018). *Les massacres de la République romaine*. Fayard, Paris.

Barrett, J., P. Freeman and A. Woodward (2000). *Cadbury Castle, Somerset*. English Heritage, London.

Becker, A. and G. Rasbach (eds.) (2015). *Waldgirmes. Die Ausgrabungen in der spätaugusteischen Siedlung von Lahnau-Waldgirmes (1993–2009)*. Philipp von Zabern, Darmstadt.

Bellón, J. P., M. A. Lechuga, C. Rueda, et al. (2021). *De situ Iliturgi*, análisis arqueológico de su asedio en el contexto de la segunda guerra púnica. *Archivo Español de Arqueología* 94: e15.

Bellón, J. P., A. Ruiz, M. Molinos, C. Rueda and F. Gómez (eds.) (2015). *La Segunda Guerra Púnica en la Península Ibérica. Baecula, arqueología de una batalla*. Universidad de Jaén, Jaén.

Beltrán, A., E. Zubiaurre, A. Orejas, L. Arboledas and J. L. Pecharromán (2019). Presencia militar en las zonas mineras del noroeste peninsular: dominio y explotación territorial. *Actes du Groupe de Recherches sur l'Esclavage depuis l'Antiquité* 38: 267–295.

Belvedere, O. and J. Bergemann (eds.) (2021). *Imperium Romanum: Romanization between Colonization and Globalization*. Palermo University Press, Palermo.

Bloxham, D. and A. D. Moses (eds.) (2010). *The Oxford Handbook of Genocide Studies*. Oxford University Press, Oxford.

Bohigas, R., E. Peralta and I. Ruiz Vélez (2015). Un nuevo gran episodio del 'Bellum Cantabricum': el cerco a Peña Dulla (merindad de Sotoscueva, Burgos). In J. Camino, E. Peralta and J. F. Torres-Martínez (eds.), *Las Guerras Astur-Cántabras*. KRK Ediciones, Gijón: 191–195.

Bourdieu, P. (1977). *Outline of a Theory of Practice*. Cambridge University Press, Cambridge.

Bourdieu, P. (1990). *The Logic of Practice*. Stanford University Press, Stanford, CA.

Bowes, K. (ed.) (2021). *The Roman Peasant Project 2009–2014*. University of Pennsylvania Press, Philadelphia, PA.

Breeze, D. (1988). Why did the Romans fail to conquer Scotland? *Proceedings of the Society of Antiquaries of Scotland* 118: 3–22.

Breeze, D. (2006). *Roman Scotland: Frontier Country*. Batsford, London.

Breeze, D. (2018). The value of studying Roman frontiers. *Theoretical Roman Archaeology Journal* 1: 1–17.

Breeze, D. (2019). Oppida in Britain in the face of the Roman conquest. In T. Romankiewicz, M. Fernández-Götz, G. Lock and O. Buchsenschutz (eds.),

Enclosing Space, Opening New Ground: Iron Age Studies from Scotland to Mainland Europe. Oxbow, Oxford: 121–128.

Breeze, D., R. Jones and I. Oltean (eds.) (2015). *Understanding Roman Frontiers.* John Donald, Edinburgh.

Brown, C. J., J. F. Torres-Martínez, M. Fernández-Götz and A. Martínez-Velasco (2017). Fought under the walls of *Bergida*: KOCOA analysis of the Roman attack on the Cantabrian *oppidum* of Monte Bernorio (Spain). *Journal of Conflict Archaeology* 12(2): 115–138.

Brun, P. and P. Ruby (2008). *L'âge du Fer en France.* La Découverte, Paris.

Büntgen, U., W. Tegel, K. Nicolussi, et al. (2011). 2500 Years of European climate variability and human susceptibility. *Science* 331: 578–582.

Burmeister, S. (2015). Roms Kampf im Norden. Die Eroberung Germaniens. In S. Burmeister and J. Rottmann (eds.), *Ich Germanicus: Feldherr, Priester, Superstar.* Theiss, Darmstadt: 9–16.

Burmeister, S. (2020). Germanen? Die Facetten und Probleme eines germanischen Kollektivbegriffs vor dem Hintergrund der bekannten Quellen. In G. Uelsberg and M. Wemhoff (eds.), *Germanen: Eine archäologische Bestandsaufnahme.* Wissenschaftliche Buchgesellschaft, Darmstadt: 417–431.

Burmeister, S. (2021). Hyper-Geschichte. Arminius und die Varusschlacht als Motor nationaler Identitätsbildung. In A. Abar, M. B. D'Anna, G. Cyrus, et al. (eds.), *Pearls, Politics and Pistachios. Essays in Anthropology and Memories on the Occasion of Susan Pollock's 65th Birthday.* Propylaeum, Heidelberg: 477–492.

Burmeister, S. (2022). Hermeneutik des Konflikts: Kalkriese als Ort der Varusschlacht. In C. Rass and M. Adam (eds.), *Konfliktlandschaften interdisziplinär lesen.* V&R unipress/Universitätsverlag Osnabrück, Göttingen: 99–129.

Cadiou, F. and M. Navarro-Caballero (eds.) (2014). *La guerre et ses traces. Conflits et sociétés en Hispanie à l'époque de la conquête romaine (IIIe-Ier s. a.C.).* Ausonius, Bordeaux.

Cahana-Blum, J. and K. MacKendrick (eds.) (2019). *We and They: Decolonizing Graeco-Roman and Biblical Antiquities.* Aarhus University Press, Aarhus.

Camino, J. (2015). La línea de operaciones de la vía Carisa. In J. Camino, E. Peralta and J. F. Torres-Martínez (eds.), *Las Guerras Astur-Cántabras.* KRK Ediciones, Gijón: 217–237.

Camino, J. and E. Martín-Hernández (2014). La Carisa, un eje de conquista en el *Bellum Asturicum*. In E. Martínez Ruiz and J. Cantera Montenegro (eds.), *Perspectivas y novedades de la historia militar.* Ministerio de Defensa, Madrid: 135–154.

Camino, J., E. Peralta and J. F. Torres-Martínez (eds.) (2015). *Las Guerras Astur-Cántabras*. KRK Ediciones, Gijón.

Carman, J. (2014). *Archaeologies of Conflict*. Bloomsbury, London.

Chalk, F. and K. Jonassohn (1990). *The History and Sociology of Genocide*. Yale University Press, New Haven, CT.

Champion, T. (2016). Britain before the Romans. In M. Millett, L. Revell and A. Moore (eds.), *The Oxford Handbook of Roman Britain*. Oxford University Press, Oxford: 150–178.

Cook, M. and L. Dunbar (2008). *Rituals, Roundhouses and Romans: Excavations at Kintore, Aberdeenshire, 2000–2006*. Scottish Trust for Archaeological Research, Edinburgh.

Costa-García, J. M. and J. García-Sánchez (in press). The siege of Cerro Castarreño. In M. Driessen, E. P. Graafstal, T. Hazenberg, et al. (eds.), *Limes XXV. Proceedings of the 25th International Congress of Roman Frontier Studies*. Sidestone Press, Leiden.

Creighton, J. (2000). *Coins and Power in Late Iron Age Britain*. Cambridge University Press, Cambridge.

Cruz, E. A. (2010). *The Grand Araucanian Wars 1541–1883 in the Kingdom of Chile*. Xlibris, Bloomington, IN.

Danieli, Y. (ed.) (1998). *International Handbook of Multigenerational Legacies of Trauma*. Plenum, New York, NY.

de Jersey, P. (2019). The island of Jersey: Focus of resistance or field of last resort? In A. Fitzpatrick and C. Haselgrove (eds.), *Julius Caesar's Battle for Gaul: New Archaeological Perspectives*. Oxbow, Oxford: 267–283.

Delibes, G., A. Esparza and R. Martín Valls (1996). *Los tesoros prerromanos de Arrabalde (Zamora) y la joyería celtibérica*. Fundación Rei Afonso Henriques, Zamora.

Deyber, A. and T. Luginbühl (2018). Cimbri and Teutones against Rome: First results concerning the battle of Arausio (105 BC). In M. Fernández-Götz and N. Roymans (eds.), *Conflict Archaeology: Materialities of Collective Violence from Prehistory to Late Antiquity*. Routledge, Abingdon: 155–166.

Dietler, M. (1994). Our ancestors the Gauls: Archaeology, ethnic nationalism, and the manipulation of Celtic identity in modern Europe. *American Anthropologist* 96: 584–605.

Dingwall, K. and J. Shepherd (2018). *Highway Through History: An Archaeological Journey on the Aberdeen Western Peripheral Route*. Headland Archaeology, Edinburgh.

Dolfini, A., R. Crellin, C. Horn and M. Uckelmann (eds.) (2018). *Prehistoric Warfare and Violence*. Springer, New York, NY.

Elkins, C. (2022). *Legacy of Violence: A History of the British Empire*. Bodley Head, London.

Fernández-Crespo, T., J. Ordoño, A. Llanos and R. Schulting (2020). Make a desert and call it peace: Massacre at the Iberian Iron Age village of La Hoya. *Antiquity* 94(377): 1245–1262.

Fernández-Götz, M. (2014). *Identity and Power: The Transformation of Iron Age Societies in Northeast Gaul*. Amsterdam University Press, Amsterdam.

Fernández-Götz, M. (2018). Urbanization in Iron Age Europe: Trajectories, patterns and social dynamics. *Journal of Archaeological Research* 26: 117–162.

Fernández-Götz, M. and B. Arnold (2019). Internal conflict in Iron Age Europe: Methodological challenges and possible scenarios. *World Archaeology* 51(5): 654–672.

Fernández-Götz, M., D. Cowley, D. Hamilton, I. Hardwick and S. McDonald (2022). Beyond walls: Reassessing Iron Age and Roman encounters in northern Britain. *Antiquity* 96(388): 1021–1029.

Fernández-Götz, M., D. Maschek and N. Roymans (2020). The dark side of the Empire: Roman expansionism between object agency and predatory regime. *Antiquity* 94(378): 1630–1639.

Fernández-Götz, M. and N. Roymans (eds.) (2018). *Conflict Archaeology: Materialities of Collective Violence from Prehistory to Late Antiquity*. Routledge, Abingdon.

Fernández-Götz, M. and N. Roymans (in press). Failed conquests: How Iron Age social structures shaped the limits of Roman expansion. In R. Witcher and E. Hanscam (eds.), *Resistance & Reception: Critical Archaeologies of Iron Age & Roman Worlds*. Archaeopress, Oxford.

Fernández-Götz, M., J. F. Torres-Martínez and A. Martínez-Velasco (2018). The battle at Monte Bernorio and the Augustan conquest of Cantabrian Spain. In M. Fernández-Götz and N. Roymans (eds.), *Conflict Archaeology: Materialities of Collective Violence from Prehistory to Late Antiquity*. Routledge, Abingdon: 127–140.

Fichtl, S. (2012). *Les peuples gaulois: IIIe-Ier siècle av. J.-C.* Errance, Paris.

Fields, N. (2020). *Britannia AD 43: The Claudian Invasion*. Osprey, Oxford.

Fitzpatrick, A. (1989). The submission of the Orkney Islands to Claudius: New evidence? *Scottish Archaeological Review* 6: 24–33.

Fitzpatrick, A. (2001). Cross-Channel exchange, Hengistbury Head and the end of hillforts. In J. Collis (ed.), *Society and Settlement in Iron Age Europe*. Sheffield Archaeological Monograph, Sheffield: 82–97.

Fitzpatrick, A. (2018). Ebbsfleet, 54 BC. *Current Archaeology* 337: 26–32.

Fitzpatrick, A. (2019). Caesar's landing sites in Britain and Gaul in 55 and 54 BC. In A. Fitzpatrick and C. Haselgrove (eds.), *Julius Caesar's Battle for Gaul: New Archaeological Perspectives*. Oxbow, Oxford: 135–158.

Fitzpatrick, A. (2023). Le casque de la fin de l'âge du Fer avec une crête en forme d'oiseau trouvé à North Bersted, West Sussex, Angleterre. In E. Warmenbol and J. Cao-Van (eds.), *Les Celtes et les oiseaux*. Carnyx 2, Libramont: 102–115.

Fitzpatrick, A. and C. Haselgrove (eds.) (2019). *Julius Caesar's Battle for Gaul: New Archaeological Perspectives*. Oxbow, Oxford.

Fitzpatrick, A. and C. Haselgrove (2023). Caesar in Britain: Britain in Rome. In J. K. Jacobsen, R. Raja and S. Grove Saxkjær (eds.), *Caesar, Rome and Beyond*. Brepols, Turnhout: 97–116.

Folkers, A., H. Jöns, S. Merkel, et al. (2018). Römisch-germanische Kontakte an der Huntemündung? Fragestellungen, Methoden und erste Ergebnisse aktueller interdisziplinärer Forschungen am Ufermarkt von Elsfleth-Hogenkamp und seinem Umfeld. In S. Burmeister and S. Ortisi (eds.), *Phantom Germanicus. Spurensuche zwischen historischer Überlieferung und archäologischem Befund*. Verlag Marie Leidorf, Rahden/Westf.: 335–360.

Fulford, M., A. Clarke, E. Durham and N. Pankhurst (2018). *Late Iron Age Calleva*. Society for the Promotion of Roman Studies, London.

Galtung, J. (1990). Cultural violence. *Journal of Peace Research* 27(3): 291–305.

García-Sánchez, J., J. M. Costa-García, J. Fonte and D. González-Álvarez (2022). Exploring ephemeral features with ground-penetrating radar: An approach to Roman military camps. *Remote Sensing* 14(19): 4884. https://doi.org/10.3390/rs14194884.

Gardner, A. (2013). Thinking about Roman imperialism: Postcolonialism, globalisation and beyond? *Britannia* 44: 1–25.

Gardner, A. (2020). Re-balancing the Romans. *Antiquity* 94(378): 1640–1642.

Garland, N. (2020). The origins of British *oppida*. *Oxford Journal of Archaeology* 39(1): 107–125.

Gillespie, C. (2018). *Boudica: Warrior Woman of Roman Britain*. Oxford University Press, Oxford.

Girault, J.-P. (2013). *La fontaine de Loulié au Puy d'Issolud. Le dossier archéologique du siège d'Uxellodunum*. Centre archéologique européen, Glux-en-Glenne.

González-Echegaray, J. (1999). Las guerras cántabras en las fuentes. In *Las Guerras Cántabras*. Fundación Marcelino Botín & Real Academia de la Historia, Santander: 145–169.

González-Ruibal, A. (2015). An archaeology of predation: Capitalism and the coloniality of power in Equatorial Guinea (Central Africa). In M. Leone and J. Knauf (eds.), *Historical Archaeologies of Capitalism*. Springer, New York, NY: 421–444.

González-Ruibal, A. and G. Moshenska (eds.) (2015). *Ethics and the Archaeology of Violence*. Springer, New York, NY.

Graafstal, E. P. (2023). Roman 'grand strategy' in action? Claudius and the annexation of Britain and Thrace. *Britannia* 54: 23–50.

Griffiths, D. (2013). *Augustus and the Roman Provinces of Iberia*. Unpublished PhD Thesis, University of Liverpool.

Hanel, N. and P. Rothenhöfer (2005). Germanisches Blei für Rom. Die Rolle des römischen Bergbaus im rechtsrheinischen Germanien im frühen Prinzipat. *Germania* 83: 53–65.

Hanson, W. S. (2007). *Elginhaugh: A Flavian Fort and its Annexe*. Society for the Promotion of Roman Studies, London.

Haselgrove, C. (ed.) (2016). *Cartimandua's Capital? The Late Iron Age Royal Site at Stanwick, North Yorkshire*. Council for British Archaeology, York.

Haselgrove, C. (2019). The Gallic War in the chronology of Iron Age coinage. In A. Fitzpatrick and C. Haselgrove (eds.), *Julius Caesar's Battle for Gaul: New Archaeological Perspectives*. Oxbow, Oxford: 241–266.

Heinrichs, J. (2008). Die Eburonen, oder: Die Kunst des Überlebens. *Zeitschrift für Papyrologie und Epigraphik* 164: 203–230.

Hierro, J. A., J. M. Vidal, E. Peralta, E. Gutiérrez and R. Bolado (2019). Primeras evidencias arqueológicas del asedio romano al castro de Las Labradas-El Marrón (Arrabalde, Zamora) durante el *Bellum Astvricum*. *Estudios Humanísticos. Historia* 17: 1–27.

Hill, J. D. (2006). Are we any closer to understanding how later Iron Age societies worked (or did not work)? In C. Haselgrove (ed.), *Celtes et Gaulois, l'Archéologie face à l'Histoire. Les mutations de la fin de l'âge du Fer*. Centre archéologique européen, Glux-en-Glenne: 169–179.

Hillman, A. L., M. B. Abbott, B. Valero-Garcés, et al. (2017). Lead pollution resulting from Roman gold extraction in northwestern Spain. *The Holocene* 27(10): 1465–1474.

Hingley, R. (2018). *Londinium: A Biography*. Bloomsbury, London.

Hingley, R. (2022). *Conquering the Ocean: The Roman Invasion of Britain*. Oxford University Press, Oxford.

Hingley, R. and C. Unwin (2005). *Boudica: Iron Age Warrior Queen*. Hambledon and London, London.

Hornung, S. (2016). *Siedlung und Bevölkerung in Ostgallien zwischen Gallischem Krieg und der Festigung der Römischen Herrschaft: Eine*

Studie auf Basis landschaftsarchäologischer Forschungen im Umfeld des Oppidums 'Hunnenring' von Otzenhausen (Lkr. St Wendel). Philipp von Zabern, Darmstadt.

Hornung, S. (2018). Tracing Julius Caesar: The Late Republican military camp at Hermeskeil and its historical context. In M. Fernández-Götz and N. Roymans (eds.), *Conflict Archaeology: Materialities of Collective Violence from Prehistory to Late Antiquity.* Routledge, Abingdon: 193–203.

Hornung, S. (2021). *Omni Gallia pacata.* Die Anfänge der römischen Herrschaft am Rhein. In E. Claßen, M. Rind, T. Schürmann and M. Trier (eds.), *Roms fliessende Grenzen.* Theiss, Darmstadt: 85–93.

James, S. (2011). *Rome & the Sword: How Warriors & Weapons Shaped Roman History.* Thames and Hudson, London.

Jiménez, A., J. Bermejo, P. Valdés, F. Moreno and K. Tardio (2020). Renewed work at the Roman camps at Renieblas near Numantia (2nd-1st c. B.C.). *Journal of Roman Archaeology* 33: 4–35.

Jones, R. (2011). *Roman Camps in Scotland.* Society of Antiquaries of Scotland, Edinburgh.

Jones, R. (2012). *Roman Camps in Britain.* Amberley, Stroud.

Kehne, P. (2017). Germanicus und die Germanenfeldzüge 10 bis 16 n.Chr. In R. Asskamp and K. Jansen (eds.), *Triumph ohne Sieg: Roms Ende in Germanien.* Philipp von Zabern, Darmstadt: 93–100.

Kehne, P. (2018). Zur Erforschung der Germanicusfeldzüge, zu den Ursachen für die Unmöglichkeit ihrer Rekonstruktion und zu den Problemen des Germanicus-Bildes. In S. Burmeister and S. Ortisi (eds.), *Phantom Germanicus: Spurensuche zwischen historischer Überlieferung und archäologischem Befund.* Verlag Marie Leidorf, Rahden/Westf.: 31–94.

Kemmers, F. (2008). Marcus Agrippa and the earliest Roman fortress at Nijmegen: The coin finds from the Hunerberg. In M. Paz García-Bellido, A. Mostalac and A. Jiménez (eds.), *Del imperium de Pompeyo a la auctoritas de Augusto. Homenaje a Michael Grant.* Consejo Superior de Investigaciones Científicas, Madrid: 165–172.

Kiernan, B. (2007). Classical genocide and early modern memory. In B. Kiernan (ed.), *Blood and Soil.* Yale University Press, New Haven, CT: 42–71.

Kiernan, B., T. M. Lemos and T. S. Taylor (eds.) (2023). *The Cambridge World History of Genocide. Volume 1: Genocide in the Ancient, Medieval and Premodern Worlds.* Cambridge University Press, Cambridge.

Kraus, C. S. (2009). Bellum Gallicum. In M. Griffin (ed.), *A Companion to Julius Caesar.* Blackwell, Oxford: 159–174.

Lamb, A. W. (2018). The Belgae of Gaul and Britain: Revisiting cross-Channel contacts in the later Iron Age. In P. Pavúk, V. Klontza-Jaklová and A. Harding (eds.), *ΕΥΔΑΙΜΩΝ. Studies in Honour of Jan Bouzek*. Charles University, Prague: 335–357.

Lange, C. H. and F. J. Vervaet (eds.) (2019). *The Historiography of the Late Republican Civil War*. Brill, Leiden.

Lavan, M. (2020). Devastation: The destruction of populations and human landscapes and the Roman imperial project. In K. Berthelot (ed.), *Reconsidering Roman Power*. Publications de l'École française de Rome, Rome: 179–205.

Lefort, A., A. Baron, F. Blondel, P. Méniel and S. Rottier (2015). Artisanat, commerce et nécropole. Un port de La Tène D1 à Urville-Nacqueville. In F. Olmer and R. Réjane (eds.), *Les Gaulois au fil de l'eau*. Ausonius, Bordeaux: 481–514.

Lodwick, L. (2014). Condiments before Claudius: New plant foods at the late Iron Age *oppidum* at Silchester, UK. *Vegetation History and Archaeobotany* 23: 543–549.

Löhr, H. (2018). Les installations militaires tardorépublicaines sur le Petrisberg à Trèves. In M. Reddé (ed.), *Les armées romaines en Gaule à l'époque republicaine*. Centre archéologique européen, Glux-en-Glenne: 135–152.

Luley, B. (2020). *Continuity and Rupture in Roman Mediterranean Gaul*. Oxbow, Oxford.

Lund, A. (1998). *Die ersten Germanen. Ethnizität und Ethnogenese*. Winter, Heidelberg.

Martín-Hernández, E., A. Martínez-Velasco, D. Díaz, F. Muñoz Villarejo and L. Bécares (2020). Castrametación romana en la Meseta Norte hispana: nuevas evidencias de recintos militares en la vertiente meridional de la cordillera Cantábrica (provincias de Burgos y Palencia). *Zephyrvs* 86: 143–164.

Maschek, D. (2018). *Die römischen Bürgerkriege: Archäologie und Geschichte einer Krisenzeit*. Philipp von Zabern, Darmstadt.

Maschek, D. (2021). How the Romans conquered and built their world, and why this matters. *Journal of Roman Archaeology* 34: 314–330.

Mata, K. (2019). *Iron Age Slaving and Enslavement in Northwest Europe*. Archaeopress, Oxford.

Mattingly, D. (2011). *Imperialism, Power, and Identity: Experiencing the Roman Empire*. Princeton University Press, Princeton, NJ.

Mbembe, A. (2001). *On the Postcolony*. University of California Press, Berkeley.

McCarthy, M. (2018). Carlisle: Function and change between the first and seventh centuries AD. *Archaeological Journal* 175(2): 292–314.

Meller, H. (ed.) (2009). *Schlachtfeldarchäologie – Battlefield Archaeology.* Landesamt für Denkmalpflege und Archäologie Sachsen-Anhalt, Halle.

Menéndez-Blanco, A., J. García-Sánchez, J. M. Costa-García, et al. (2020). Following the Roman army between the southern foothills of the Cantabrian Mountains and the northern plains of Castile and León (North of Spain). *Geosciences* 10(12): 485. https://doi.org/10.3390/geosciences10120485.

Metzler, J., C. Gaeng, P. Méniel, et al. (2018). Comptoir commercial italique et occupation militaire romaine dans l'oppidum du Titelberg. In M. Reddé (ed.), *L'armée romaine en Gaule à l'époque républicaine.* Centre archéologique européen, Glux-en-Glenne: 179–205.

Meyer, M. (2013). Rhein-Weser-Germanen. Bemerkungen zur Genese und Interpretation. In G. Rasbach (ed.), *Westgermanische Bodenfunde.* Römisch-Germanische Kommission, Frankfurt: 31–38.

Meyer, M. (2018). The Germanic-Roman battlefields of Kalkriese and Harzhorn. In M. Fernández-Götz and N. Roymans (eds.), *Conflict Archaeology: Materialities of Collective Violence from Prehistory to Late Antiquity.* Routledge, Abingdon: 205–217.

Mignolo, W. (2011). *The Darker Side of Western Modernity.* Duke University Press, Durham.

Millett, M. and T. Wilmott (2003). Rethinking Richborough. In P. Wilson (ed.), *The Archaeology of Roman Towns.* Oxbow, Oxford: 184–194.

Moosbauer, G. (2009). *Die Varusschlacht.* Beck, Munich.

Moosbauer, G. (2018). *Die vergessene Römerschlacht: Der sensationelle Fund am Harzhorn.* Beck, Munich.

Morillo, A. (2014). Arqueología de la conquista del Norte peninsular. Nuevas interpretaciones sobre las campañas 26–25 a. C. In F. Cadiou and M. Navarro-Caballero (eds.), *La guerre et ses traces. Conflits et sociétés en Hispanie à l'époque de la conquête romaine (IIIe-Ier s. a.C.).* Ausonius, Bordeaux: 133–148.

Morillo, A. (2017). El periodo de la 'Paz Armada' en el norte de Hispania (19/ 15 a.C.-15/20 d.C.): ¿la creación de un sistema de defensa sin frontera? *Gerión* 35: 191–223.

Morillo, A., A. M. Adroher, M. Dobson and E. Martín-Hernández (2020). Constructing the archaeology of the Roman conquest of *Hispania*: New evidence, perspectives and challenges. *Journal of Roman Archaeology* 33: 36–52.

Morillo, A. and F. Sala (2019). The Sertorian Wars in the conquest of Hispania: From data to archaeological assessment. In A. Fitzpatrick and C. Haselgrove (eds.), *Julius Caesar's Battle for Gaul: New Archaeological Perspectives*. Oxbow, Oxford: 49–72.

Morley, N. (2010). *The Roman Empire: Roots of Imperialism*. Pluto Press, London.

Noguera, J., E. Ble and P. Valdés (2013). *La Segona Guerra Púnica al nord-est d'Ibèria*. Societat Catalana d'Arqueologia, Barcelona.

Noguera, J., P. Valdés and E. Ble (2022). New perspectives on the Sertorian War in northeastern Hispania. *Journal of Roman Archaeology* 35: 1–32.

Nüsse, H.-J. (2014). *Haus, Gehöft und Siedlung im Norden und Westen der Germania Magna*. Verlag Marie Leidorf, Rahden/Westf.

Padilla Peralta, D. (2020). Epistemicide: The Roman case. *Classica* 33(2): 151–186.

Paridaens, N. (2020). L'oppidum du 'Bois du Grand Bon Dieu' à Thuin. Résultats des recherches 2018–2019. *LUNULA* 28: 145–148.

Paridaens, N., K. Salesse, R. Müller, et al. (2020). Les balles de fronde en plomb découvertes sur l'oppidum de Thuin. *Signa* 9: 111–123.

Peralta, E. (2001). Die augusteische Belagerung von La Espina del Gallego (Kantabrien, Spanien). *Germania* 79: 21–42.

Peralta, E. (2003). *Los Cántabros antes de Roma*. Real Academia de la Historia, Madrid.

Peralta, E. (2004). La conquista romana de Campoo: arqueología de las guerras cántabras. *Cuadernos de Campoo* 36: 28–42.

Peralta, E. (2015). El asedio de La Loma (Santibáñez de La Peña, Palencia) y otros campamentos romanos del norte de Castilla. In J. Camino, E. Peralta and J. F. Torres-Martínez (eds.), *Las Guerras Astur-Cántabras*. KRK Ediciones, Gijón: 91–109.

Peralta, E., J. Camino and J. F. Torres-Martínez (2019). Recent research on the Cantabrian Wars: The archaeological reconstruction of a mountain war. *Journal of Roman Archaeology* 32: 421–438.

Peralta, E., J. F. Torres-Martínez and S. Domínguez-Solera (2022). *Asedio de La Loma (Santibáñez de la Peña). Historia de las campañas de 2003 a 2018*. Clan Editorial, Madrid.

Perea Yébenes, S. (2017). *Triumphatores ex Hispania* (36–26 a.C.) según los *Fasti Triumphales*. *Gerión* 35: 121–149.

Pernet, L. (2019). Fighting for Caesar. The archaeology and history of Gallic auxiliaries in the 2nd-1st centuries BC. In A. Fitzpatrick and C. Haselgrove (eds.), *Julius Caesar's Battle for Gaul: New Archaeological Perspectives*. Oxbow, Oxford: 179–199.

Polak, M. and L. Kooistra (2013). A sustainable frontier? The establishment of the Roman frontier in the Rhine Delta. *Jahrbuch des Römisch-Germanischen Zentralmuseums* 60: 355–458.

Pollard, T. and I. Banks (eds.) (2005). *Past Tense: Studies in the Archaeology of Conflict*. Brill, Leiden.

Posluschny, A. and S. Schade-Lindig (2019). Bergbau und Metallwirtschaft in der ausgehenden Latène- und der augusteischen Zeit östlich des Rheins. In S. Bödecker, E. Cott, M. Brüggler, et al. (eds.), *Spätlatène- und frühkaiserzeitliche Archäologie zwischen Maas und Rhein*. LVR-Amt für Bodendenkmalpflege im Rheinland, Bonn: 193–208.

Poux, M. (2004). *L'âge du vin. Rites de boisson, festins et libations en Gaule indépendante*. Éditions Monique Mergoil, Montagnac.

Poux, M. (ed.) (2008). *Sur les traces de César: militaria tardo-républicains en contexte gaulois*. Centre archéologique européen, Glux-en-Glenne.

Pujol, A., M. Fernández-Götz, R. Sala, et al. (2019). Archaeology of the Roman Civil Wars: The destruction of Puig Ciutat (Catalonia, Spain) and Caesar's campaign in *Ilerda* (49 BC). In A. Fitzpatrick and C. Haselgrove (eds.), *Julius Caesar's Battle for Gaul: New Archaeological Perspectives*. Oxbow, Oxford: 227–240.

Quesada, F. (2019). El ejército romano en la Península Ibérica: nuevos hallazgos y líneas de investigación (1997–2017). *Índice Histórico Español* 132: 121–167.

Quesada, F. (2021). El contexto cronológico e histórico de la destrucción del asentamiento ibérico en el Cerro de la Cruz (Almedinilla, Córdoba). *Boletín de la Asociación Española de Amigos de la Arqueología* 51: 166–211.

Quesada, F. and J. Moralejo-Ordax (2020). Tras las huellas de Julio César: los campos de batalla cesarianos de *Ulia*/Montemayor y el hallazgo de un carro de época ibérica. In *Actualidad de la investigación arqueológica en España II (2019–2020)*. Museo Arqueológico Nacional, Madrid: 229–252.

Raaflaub, K. A. (ed.) (2017). *The Landmark Julius Caesar*. Pantheon Books, New York, NY.

Raaflaub, K. A. (2021). Caesar and genocide: Confronting the dark side of Caesar's Gallic Wars. *New England Classical Journal* 48(1): 54–80.

Ralston, I. (2019). The Gauls on the eve of the Roman conquest. In A. Fitzpatrick and C. Haselgrove (eds.), *Julius Caesar's Battle for Gaul: New Archaeological Perspectives*. Oxbow, Oxford: 19–47.

Ramos, F. and F. Jiménez (2015). Estrategia y logística de la conquista de la cornisa cantábrica, una operación previa a la campaña sobre la Gran Germania. In J. Camino, E. Peralta and J.F. Torres-Martínez (eds.), *Las Guerras Astur-Cántabras*. KRK Ediciones, Gijón: 305–321.

Reddé, M. (2018a). The battlefield of *Alesia*. In M. Fernández-Götz and N. Roymans (eds.), *Conflict Archaeology: Materialities of Collective Violence from Prehistory to Late Antiquity*. Routledge, Abingdon: 183–191.

Reddé, M. (ed.) (2018b). *L'armée romaine en Gaule à l'époque républicaine*. Centre archéologique européen, Glux-en-Glenne.

Reddé, M. (2019). Recent archaeological research on Roman military engineering works of the Gallic War. In A. Fitzpatrick and C. Haselgrove (eds.), *Julius Caesar's Battle for Gaul: New Archaeological Perspectives*. Oxbow, Oxford: 91–112.

Reddé, M. (2022). *Gallia Comata: La Gaule du Nord de l'indépendance à l'Empire romain*. Presses Universitaires de Rennes, Rennes.

Reddé, M. and S. von Schnurbein (eds.) (2001). *Alésia. Fouilles et recherches franco-allemandes sur les travaux militaires romains autour du Mont-Auxois (1991–1997)*. L'Académie des Inscriptions et Belles-Lettres, Paris

Redfern, R. (2011). A re-appraisal of the evidence for violence in the Late Iron Age human remains from Maiden Castle Hillfort, Dorset, England. *Proceedings of the Prehistoric Society* 77: 111–138.

Redfern, R. (2020). Iron Age 'predatory landscapes': A bioarchaeological and funerary exploration of captivity and enslavement in Britain. *Cambridge Archaeological Journal* 30(4): 531–554.

Reid, J. (2023). *The Eagle and the Bear: A New History of Roman Scotland*. Birlinn, Edinburgh.

Reid, J., R. Müller and S. Klein (2022). The Windridge Farm *glandes* revisited. *Britannia* 53: 323–346.

Reid, J. and A. Nicholson (2019). Burnswark Hill: The opening shot of the Antonine reconquest of Scotland? *Journal of Roman Archaeology* 32: 459–477.

Revell, L. (2009). *Roman Imperialism and Local Identities*. Cambridge University Press, Cambridge.

Richmond, I. (1968). *Hod Hill Volume 2*. British Museum, London.

Riggsby, A. (2006). *Caesar in Gaul and Rome: War in Words*. University of Texas Press, Austin, TX.

Rost, A. and S. Wilbers-Rost (2018). Die Knochengruben auf dem Oberesch in Kalriese – zum Spannungsverhältnis zwischen archäologischem Befund und antiken Schriftquellen. In S. Burmeister and S. Ortisi (eds.), *Phantom Germanicus: Spurensuche zwischen historischer Überlieferung und archäologischem Befund*. Verlag Marie Leidorf, Rahden/Westf: 147–160.

Roymans, N. (1990). *Tribal Societies in Northern Gaul. An Anthropological Perspective*. Universiteit van Amsterdam, Amsterdam.

Roymans, N. (2004). *Ethnic Identity and Imperial Power: The Batavians in the Early Roman Empire*. Amsterdam University Press, Amsterdam.

Roymans, N. (2011). Ethnic recruitment, returning veterans and the diffusion of Roman culture among rural populations in the Rhineland frontier zone. In N. Roymans and T. Derks (eds.), *Villa Landscapes in the Roman North*. Amsterdam University Press, Amsterdam: 139–160.

Roymans, N. (2018). A Roman massacre in the far north. Caesar's annihilation of the Tencteri and Usipetes in the Dutch River area. In M. Fernández-Götz and N. Roymans (eds.), *Conflict Archaeology: Materialies of Collective Violence from Prehistory to Late Antiquity*. Routledge, Abingdon: 167–181.

Roymans, N. (2019a). Conquest, mass violence and ethnic stereotyping. Investigating Caesar's actions in the Germanic frontier zone. *Journal of Roman Archaeology* 32: 439–458.

Roymans, N. (2019b). Late Iron Age coin hoards with silver rainbow staters from Graetheide (NL) and the mid-1st century BC hoard horizon in the Lower Rhine / Meuse region. *Germania* 97: 65–92.

Roymans, N. (2023). The Cimbrian migration conceived as an expression of societal stress caused by soil degradation in the Northwest-European Plain. In V. Guichard (ed.), *Continuités et discontinuités à la fin du IIe siècle avant notre ère dans l'espace celtique et à sa périphérie*. Centre archéologique européen, Glux-en-Glenne: 227–240.

Roymans, N. (in prep.). *Ethnic Recruitment and the Genesis of the Batavians as a Soldiering People: The Numismatic Evidence*. Amsterdam.

Roymans, N. and M. Fernández-Götz (2018). The archaeology of warfare and mass violence in ancient Europe. An introduction. In M. Fernández-Götz and N. Roymans (eds.), *Conflict Archaeology: Materialies of Collective Violence from Prehistory to Late Antiquity*. Routledge, Abingdon: 1–10.

Roymans, N. and M. Fernández-Götz (2019). Reconsidering the Roman conquest: New archaeological perspectives. *Journal of Roman Archaeology* 32: 415–420.

Roymans, N. and M. Fernández-Götz (2023). The archaeology of Julius Caesar: New research on the Gallic Wars. In J.K. Jacobsen, R. Raja and S. Grove Saxkjær (eds.), *Caesar, Rome and Beyond*. Brepols, Turnhout: 51–69.

Roymans, N. and D. Habermehl (2023). Migration and ethnic dynamics in the Lower Rhine frontier zone of the expanding Roman Empire (60 BC-AD 20): A historical-anthropological perspective. In M. Fernández-Götz, C. Nimura, P. Stockhammer and R. Cartwright (eds.), *Rethinking Migrations in Late Prehistoric Eurasia*. Oxford University Press, Oxford: 292–312.

Roymans, N. and S. Scheers (2012). Eight gold hoards from the Low Countries. A synthesis. In N. Roymans, G. Creemers and S. Scheers, S. (eds.), *Late Iron Age Gold Hoards from the Low Countries and the Caesarian Conquest of Northern Gaul*. Amsterdam University Press, Amsterdam: 1–46.

Rudnick, B. (2017). Die Germanenkriege des Augustus 12 v. bis 10 n.Chr. in der archäologischen Überlieferung. In R. Asskamp and K. Jansen (eds.), *Triumph ohne Sieg. Roms Ende in Germanien*. Philipp von Zabern, Darmstadt: 81–92.

Ruiz Zapatero, G. (2016). Los pueblos prerromanos al servicio de la Dictadura Franquista (1939–1956). In F. J. Moreno Martín (ed.), *El franquismo y la apropiación del pasado*. Editorial Pablo Iglesias, Madrid: 45–66.

Russell, M. (2019). Mythmakers of Maiden Castle: Breaking the siege mentality of an Iron Age hillfort. *Oxford Journal of Archaeology* 38(3): 325–342.

Sánchez-Palencia, F. J. (ed.) (2000). *Las Médulas (León)*. Instituto Leonés de Cultura, León.

Santos, B. de Sousa (2016). Epistemologies of the South and the future. *From the European South* 1: 17–29.

Sauer, E. (2002). The Roman invasion of Britain (AD 43) in imperial perspective. *Oxford Journal of Archaeology* 21(4): 333–363.

Sauer, E., N. Cooper, G. Dannell, et al. (2000). Alchester, a Claudian 'vexillation fortress' near the western boundary of the Catuvellauni: New light on the Roman invasion of Britain. *Archaeological Journal* 157(1): 1–78.

Saunders, N. (ed.) (2012). *Beyond the Dead Horizon: Studies in Modern Conflict Archaeology*. Oxbow, Oxford.

Schallmayer, E. (2011). *Der Limes: Geschichte einer Grenze*. Beck, Munich.

Scheper-Hughes, N. and P. Bourgois (eds.) (2004). *Violence in War and Peace*. Blackwell, Oxford.

Schulze-Forster, J. (2002). *Die latènezeitliche Funde vom Dünsberg*. Unpublished PhD Thesis, Philipps-Universität Marburg.

Scott, D., L. Babits and C. Haecker (eds.) (2009). *Fields of Conflict: Battlefield Archaeology from the Roman Empire to the Korean War*. Potomac Books, Washington, DC.

Scott, D., R. Fox, M. Connor and D. Harmon (1989). *Archaeological Perspectives on the Battle of the Little Bighorn*. University of Oklahoma Press, Norman, OK.

Scott, D. and A. P. McFeaters (2011). The archaeology of historic battlefields. *Journal of Archaeological Research* 19: 103–132.

Setién, J. and M. Cisneros (2023). Archeometrical study of metallic remains from 'La Ulaña' archeological site. *Metallography, Microstructure, and Analysis* 12: 327–348.

Sharples, N. (2014). Are the developed hillforts of southern England urban? In M. Fernández-Götz, H. Wendling and K. Winger (eds.), *Paths to Complexity: Centralisation and Urbanisation in Iron Age Europe*. Oxbow, Oxford: 224–232.

Shaw, B. D. (in press). The exterminating angel: The Roman imperial state and its indigenous peoples. In F. Yarbrough and M. Maas (eds.), *States and Their Indigenous Peoples*. University of Oklahoma Press, Norman.

Siegmüller, A. (2018). Zeiten des Umbruchs. Landschaftsveränderungen um Christi Geburt im Emsmündungsgebiet und die Folgen für die Siedlungsstrukturen. In S. Burmeister and S. Ortisi (eds.), *Phantom Germanicus: Spurensuche zwischen historischer Überlieferung und archäologischem Befund*. Verlag Marie Leidorf, Rahden/Westf.: 319–333.

Silva-Sánchez, N. and X.-L. Armada (2023). Environmental impact of Roman mining and metallurgy and its correlation with the archaeological evidence: A European perspective. *Environmental Archaeology*. https://doi.org/10.1080/14614103.2023.2181295.

Slofstra, J. (2002). Batavians and Romans on the Lower Rhine: The Romanisation of a frontier area. *Archaeological Dialogues* 9: 16–38 & 55–57.

Snodgrass, A. (2017). Urbanism: A view from the south. In S. Stoddart (ed.), *Delicate Urbanism in Context: Settlement Nucleation in Pre-Roman Germany*. McDonald Institute Monographs, Cambridge: 115–116.

Stewart, D., P. Cheetham and M. Russell (2020). A magnetometry survey of the Second Augustan Legionary fortress at Lake Farm, Dorset. *Britannia* 51: 307–317.

Taylor, T. S. (2023). Caesar's Gallic genocide. A case study in ancient mass violence. In B. Kiernan, T. M. Lemos and T. S. Taylor (eds.), *The Cambridge World History of Genocide: Volume 1: Genocide in the Ancient, Medieval and Premodern Worlds*. Cambridge University Press, Cambridge: 309–329.

Thurston, T. L. and M. Fernández-Götz (eds.) (2021). *Power from Below in Premodern Societies: The Dynamics of Political Complexity in the Archaeological Record*. Cambridge University Press, Cambridge.

Torres-Martínez, J. F., M. Fernández-Götz, A. Martínez-Velasco and D. Vacas (2019). La romanización de la Montaña Palentina: el yacimiento hispano-romano de la Huerta Varona (Aguilar de Campoo). *Colección de Historia de la Montaña Palentina* 11: 155–214.

Torres-Martínez, J. F., M. Fernández-Götz, A. Martínez-Velasco, D. Vacas and E. Rodríguez-Millán (2016). From the Bronze Age to the Roman conquest: The oppidum of Monte Bernorio (northern Spain). *Proceedings of the Prehistoric Society* 82: 363–382.

Torrione, M. (2018). Dessobriga: *oppidum* vacceo, *mansio* altoimperial . . . una búsqueda en curso. In C. Sanz Mínguez and J. F. Blanco García (eds.), *Novedades arqueológicas en cuatro ciudades vacceas*. Centro de Estudios Vacceos Federico Wattenberg, Valladolid: 31–48.

Torrione, M. and S. Cahanier (2014). Una moneda gala en el horizonte de las Guerras Cántabras. *Sautuola* 19: 283–298.

Van Wees, H. (2010). Genocide in the ancient world. In D. Bloxham and A. D. Moses (eds.), *The Oxford Handbook of Genocide Studies*. Oxford University Press, Oxford: 239–258.

Von See, K. (1981). Der Germane als Barbar. *Jahrbuch für Internationale Germanistik* 13: 42–72.

Wallace, L. (2016). The early Roman horizon. In M. Millett, L. Revell and A. Moore (eds.), *The Oxford Handbook of Roman Britain*. Oxford University Press, Oxford: 117–133.

Webster, J. (1999). At the end of the world: Druidic and other revitalization movements in post-conquest Gaul and Britain. *Britannia* 30: 1–20.

Wells, P. S. (2003). *The Battle that Stopped Rome*. Norton, New York, NY.

Wilbers-Rost, S. and A. Rost (2012). *Kalkriese 6. Die Verteilung der Kleinfunde auf dem Oberesch in Kalkriese*. Römisch-Germanische Forschungen 70, Mainz.

Wilbers-Rost, S. and A. Rost (2015). Looting and scrapping at the ancient battlefield of Kalkriese (9 A.D.). In J. P. Bellón, A. Ruiz, M. Molinos, C. Rueda and F. Gómez (eds.), *La Segunda Guerra Púnica en la Península Ibérica: Baecula, arqueología de una batalla*. Universidad de Jaén, Jaén: 639–650.

Wolters, R. (2017). *Die Schlacht im Teutoburger Wald*. Beck, Munich.

Woolf, G. (2011). *Tales of the Barbarians*. Wiley-Blackwell, Chichester.

Woolf, G. (2019). The Gallic Wars in Roman history. In A. Fitzpatrick and C. Haselgrove (eds.), *Julius Caesar's Battle for Gaul: New Archaeological Perspectives*. Oxbow, Oxford: 9–18.

Woolf, G. (2022). *Rome: An Empire's Story*. Oxford University Press, Oxford.

Woolliscroft, D. J. and B. Hoffmann (2006). *Rome's First Frontier: The Flavian Occupation of Northern Scotland*. Tempus, Stroud.

Zelle, M. (2015). Arminius – Cheruskerfürst und deutscher Held. In D. Boschung, A. W. Busch and M. J. Versluys (eds.), *Re-Inventing the Invention of Tradition. Indigenous Pasts and the Roman Present*. Morphomata 32, Paderborn: 45–66.

Žižek, S. (2008). *Violence*. Profile Books, London.

Acknowledgements

We would like to thank several colleagues who have provided images and/or feedback for various sections within the volume: David Breeze, Juan Pedro Bellón, Ian Ralston, Michel Reddé, Sabine Hornung, Fernando Quesada, José Manuel Costa-García, Jesús García-Sánchez, Margarita Torrione, Jesús Francisco Torres-Martínez, Stefan Burmeister, Andrew Fitzpatrick, Courtney Nimura, Richard Hingley, Christina Unwin, John Reid, Niall Sharples, Rebecca Jones, and Gabriele Rasbach. Special thanks go to Rachel Cartwright and Bettina Arnold for their editorial assistance, as well as to Bert Brouwenstijn for helping to produce the site distribution maps. Research on the topic also benefited from the support of the Philip Leverhulme Prize (PLP-2016–104).

About the Authors

Manuel Fernández-Götz is Abercromby Professor of Archaeology at the University of Edinburgh. His research focuses on Iron Age and Roman societies in Europe, with a particular interest in questions of social identities, early urbanisation, and conflict archaeology. He has directed fieldwork projects in Spain, Germany, the United Kingdom, and Croatia.

Nico Roymans is Emeritus Professor of European Archaeology at the Vrije Universiteit Amsterdam. His research focuses on Iron Age and Roman societies, with a special interest in the study of social identities, conflict archaeology, landscape archaeology, and Iron Age coinage. He has directed many large, externally funded research projects.

Cambridge Elements ☰

The Archaeology of Europe

Manuel Fernández-Götz

University of Edinburgh

Manuel Fernández-Götz is Abercromby Professor of Archaeology at the University of Edinburgh. His research focuses on Iron Age and Roman societies in Europe, with a particular interest in questions of social identities, early urbanisation, and conflict archaeology. He has directed fieldwork projects in Spain, Germany, the United Kingdom, and Croatia.

Bettina Arnold

University of Wisconsin–Milwaukee

Bettina Arnold is a Full Professor of Anthropology at the University of Wisconsin–Milwaukee and Adjunct Curator of European Archaeology at the Milwaukee Public Museum. Her research interests include the archaeology of alcohol, the archaeology of gender, mortuary archaeology, Iron Age Europe, and the history of archaeology.

About the Series

Elements in the Archaeology of Europe is a collaborative publishing venture between Cambridge University Press and the European Association of Archaeologists. Composed of concise, authoritative, and peer-reviewed studies by leading scholars, each volume in this series will provide timely, accurate, and accessible information about the latest research into the archaeology of Europe from the Paleolithic era onwards, as well as on heritage preservation.

E
A   European Association
A   *of* Archaeologists

Cambridge Elements ≡

The Archaeology of Europe

Printed in the United States
by Baker & Taylor Publisher Services